Book 1
Fortran Crash Course
By PG WIZARD BOOKS

&

Book 2
Hacking
By PG WIZARD BOOKS

&

Book 3
Android Crash Course
By PG WIZARD BOOKS

&

Book 4
Python Crash Course
By PG WIZARD BOOKS

&

Book 5
XML Crash Course
By PG WIZARD BOOKS

Book 1
Fortran Crash Course

By: PG WIZARD BOOKS

Step By Step Guide To Mastering Fortran Programming!

Fortran Crash Course: Step By Step Guide To Mastering Fortran Programming!

Fortran Crash Course: Step By Step Guide To Mastering Fortran Programming!

Table of Contents

Introduction

Many beginners to coding worry that they are not going to be able to learn how to work with a new coding language. They feel that it is going to be too difficult to learn the language and that they will either not be able to do some of the programming that they want or that they just won't understand what is being said in the information. But when it comes to working with Fortran, you will find that learning how to code is a simple process.

In this guidebook, we are going to start out by talking about some of the information that comes with Fortran. We will also work on the first code for this language and discuss all the different parts that are going to be found inside of your code. This is a simple introduction to help you get some practice with writing your own code and ensures that you are able to get into some of the more complex situations that we will discuss later on.

Once we have these basics down, we are going to move on to some of the other things that you are able to do when it comes to working on your code in Fortran. We will take a look at writing some of your own loop statements, what strings and arrays are, working with conditional statements, and so much more. Even as a beginner, you will be able to use these options in order to make a really strong code and program as you want it.

When you are ready to get into coding and want to make sure that you are designing something that is strong and will work the way that you want, Fortran is one of the best coding languages to help you learn how to get it done. Make sure to use this guidebook to help you to get the basics to work with Fortran for all your coding needs.

Chapter 1: Learning the Basics of Fortran

As a beginner, you may have times that you are worried that a new coding language will be too hard for you to learn. You want to make your own programs, learn how to work in different operating systems, or have another goal that you would like to accomplish, but you worry that it is going to be too much work for you to accomplish because it will be too hard to do. But when it comes to learning how to work with Fortran (which is basically a contraction of Formula Translation), you are working with a great language that is designed for beginners, even for those that have no experience in coding before.

Fortran is considered one of the oldest programming languages that you can use and this can be a benefit as well as an issue. It is beneficial because you will be able to find this language anywhere that you want to look and the compiler, as well as the other add-ons, are all going to be free. It is a coding language that many scientists and engineers like to use because of all the functions that are built in and the fact that it is easily used with mathematical constructs. There are also many other things that you are able to do with this coding language, and since it is one of the oldest options around, you are sure to find lots of help and answers to ensure that you get the project done right.

What will I need to get started?

When you are ready to get started with Fortran, you will need to bring out a new text editor. There are several of these that are available, and you can choose the one that works for you. You need this because it allows you to out the codes so that the compiler, which you will need next, will be able to read out what you are doing and tell the computer how to behave. You are not able to use a word processor for this because these kinds of applications are not going to save files in plain text, which is required to make the compiler do its job.

Next on the list is the compiler. There are many options out there and most of them are going to be free as well so you can download these and not have to worry about adding in costs. Basically the compiler is going to take the words that you have written in the text editor and then change them around into something that the computer is actually able to read. You will just need to save your code and then the compiler will be able to execute it.

Some people find that working with an Integrated Development Environment, or IDE, is a great way to help make this a lot easier. This IDE is going to work similar to the text editor and the compiler in one so it saves you some time, especially when it comes to troubleshooting the written code. For those who are working on Windows computers, the IDE is really a good idea because it has an interface that is easy to sue and similar to what you are used to seeing on the Windows computer.

As mentioned, you could just use the text editor and the compiler, but the IDE does make it a bit easier to write your code. These combine both of the other two products in one and it is able to understand syntaxes of the code easily. In fact, it is going to be able to catch some of the errors that come up in the code as you are typing, saving a lot of time and accidents in the process.

The benefits of using Fortran for your coding

There are so many reasons why you may want to consider using Fortran as your coding language of choice. Whether you are looking to use it on the side as another coding language to master or this is one of the first coding languages that you are going to work with, the benefits of choosing this one are amazing. Some of the reasons that you would want to work with the Fortran coding language include:

- Easy to use: Fortran was designed for the beginner to learn how to use it. It is a simple language to work with and after looking at some of the codes in this book, you are sure to see that it is easy enough to learn how to work with.
- Has been around for a long time: Fortran is one of the first coding languages that came available for coders to use in their homes. This is a good thing because it is simplistic and easy to use. We are going to work on a few different codes inside of this guidebook and you will find that most of them are pretty straight forward and easy to write, even if you are a beginner. While some people feel that the fact that Fortran has been around for so long is a bad thing, it can mean so many good things for helping you to get the very best when working in coding.

- Great for the scientific community: this is a language that anyone is able to use for their own needs, but it is specifically important when it comes to the scientific community. If you have an occupation that is in this field, you will find that it is a good idea to learn how to use the Fortran code.
- Lots of programs still use it: even though this is an older coding language that you can use, there are still a lot of programs that use it. This means that you will have plenty of chances to use this programming language and to get some more practice.
- Can be modified for other languages: Fortran is one of the earliest coding languages that is out there so it has had many adaptations over the years. This means that there are versions that you are able to use and combine with some of your other programming languages. This makes it easier to do some of the more powerful things that you want to do with your coding.
- It is free: all the stuff that you need for Fortran, from the software itself to the IDE that you want to use with it, is all free to use. This makes it easier for everyone to use this language because you won't have to worry about all the costs that are associated with it.
- Has a big community: when it comes to using a brand new language, you want to make sure that you have a community that is able to answer your questions and make sure that you going on the right track. Since Fortran has been around for so long, there are many people who know how to use this and can be there to help you out.

There are many benefits to using the Fortran coding language. While some people prefer to go with another option that is easier or newer to use, there are still many people who want to work with Fortran because it is one of the first. It is a simplistic language to learn how to use even as a beginner, and it is able to get a lot of the coding and programming done that you would like. If you are looking for a coding language that is pretty easy to work with and is meant for beginners, you won't go wrong when choosing Fortran.

How to test my first code

Now that we have spent some time talking about the things that you need to get started with the Fortran coding, it is time to test out one of our first codes. Once you have taken the time to install the IDE that you would like to use, it is time to double click on the icon so that the programming environment is going to open up. You can then create a brand new file but keep in mind that you may need to select on a Fortran file when you do this, just in case the IDE that you picked is able to read more than one language. So you will need to give it the extension of .f95 rather than of .txt so that you are able to compile these statements a bit later on.

One thing to keep in mind is that there are some other extensions that you are able to use when it comes to Fortran including .FOR, .F, and FPP. These extensions are going to tell the compiler was standards you are following with the work you do so make sure that you pick the one that you want and stick with it. You can experiment a bit to figure out which one you want to use.

So once you are done picking out the extension that you would like to use (we are going to stick with the .f95 one for now), we are going to need to type out the following code to get started:

```
program mytest

!this is a test

Print *, 'This is an output test'

end program mytest
```

After we have taken the time to type out this bit of code, it is time to execute it inside of the IDE. Your compiler will then go through and double check the parts of the code, looking to see if you have made any errors in the code before trying to run it. If there are any errors that show up, the IDE will let you know and ask you to fix it. If there aren't any troubles with the code, the compiler is going to generate and then execute the file. Basically, with this one you are going to find that the words "This is an output test" will show up on the screen if you typed it in the right way.

Breaking down this code

Now that we have taken some time to write our own code, it is time to break it down to make a bit more sense. Like a lot of the other coding languages that are out there, the Fortran language is going to take care of the different lines of the code, which are called statements, and then decide what it is going to do with each of them. So in the first line, the program is going to state the name of the program that you are trying to work with.

Then moving on to the second line, you are working with a comment. This basically means that you are writing a little note for yourself or for the other programmers that are taking a look at the code. The compiler knows that it shouldn't execute the comment since this is just a little note. You can add in as many comments as you would like inside of the code to describe what the different parts are going to do.

The third line of the code is the output command that is going to tell the compiler what it is supposed to display on the screen. It is going to show up in a single quote. You can make this statement as long or short as you would like, just make sure that you are using the right options with it. And then in the last line, the statement is terminating, or ending, the program that you just write.

Now, this is a pretty basic option that we are working on and only has four lines. There are many options that you are able to do with Fortran that will use more lines to get it done depending on the things that you are doing inside the code. There are also a few versions of Fortran that will have the code look a bit different. Basically all of them need to have the four same parts including the program name, the output statements (you may have more than one of these in some cases), end of program, and comments if you need them.

Making sure that you have all the right parts in place in order to write the code is important to helping the compiler to work with you on creating the code. And while there are many different data types that you are able to use, as we will discuss as we go on in this guidebook, they can be as simple or as difficult as you need to make the code work.

Chapter 2: Working on Loops in Fortran

When you are working on writing your own code inside of Fortran, you need to understand how to work with loops. There are many different times when you will want the code to keep repeating something, or do a specific action more than once. With the most basic form of your code, you would need to write this part of the code over and over again. Now, if you just want the code to repeat a few times, this may not seem like such a big deal, but what happens when you want to write out the code 100 times? Rewriting the same part 100 times can get tiring and old pretty quickly.

But with loops, you are able to tell the compiler to repeat the same steps until the conditions are no longer true. This could be five times and it could be 1000 times, but you would just need to write out a few lines of code to make this happen. Rather than having to write out the same instructions over and over again, you are able to set up the loop to do the same functions over and over again.

There are several different components that are going to be found inside of a loop to make sure that it is going to work. The main components include:

- Step: this component is going to tell the compiler that the procedure will need to be repeated at least once.
- Start: this is going to tell the compiler that it is at the beginning of your loop.
- Stop: this is going to tell the compiler that it is at the end of your loop.
- Var: this is a variable. It is in charge of telling the compiler how many times that you would need to have your code repeated.

How do these loops work?

Loops are going to begin when you set the start and then you define the var. they will explore what concept you are working with inside the var and decide when the conditions have no longer been met so this will all start. As soon as your statement is executed once, the amount to the var is going to go up by one so that you don't end up in an endless loop. So, if you want to make a table that goes from one to ten, the var would start at one and then each time it goes up by one until it reaches ten. Let's take a look at a sample code that shows how the loop function is going to work:

```
program loop_factorial

implicit none


        !definition of variables

        Integer::xfact=1

        Integer::x


        !computations of factorials

        Do x=1, 15

                Xfact=xfact*1

                Write*, x, xfact

        End do

End program loop_factorial
```

This one is a bit longer than what we are used to with the other code we wrote, but it does show how the loop is going to work for you. This one is going to make sure that the variable will keep going up by one each time that you work with it, helping to keep things organized and to ensure that you don't end up in an endless loop. If you do end up with a loop that doesn't have a stop point, you are going to get stuck inside of the code and have trouble getting out without closing the whole program.

There are a few different types of loops that you are able to work with. Some are going to check the conditions of the statement before determining whether or not to run the loop. If the conditions are not true from the beginning, you are not going to get the loop to run at all and it is going to head on to the next part of the code. This is known as the for loop. And then the do while loop is going to run the loop at least one time, and then run check the options to see if it meets the condition. The choice can be the same, but it does depend on whether you want the code to run one time or it doesn't matter.

The loop is one of the best things that you can work with when trying to make your code look nice and organized when on Fortran. You will be able to tell the loop how many times you would like it to run through the program, just using a few lines rather than rewriting the code all of the time. This is an efficient way to work inside of your code and ensures that the code is still able to work properly.

Chapter 3: Working with Strings and Arrays

When you are working with Fortran, you will find that strings and arrays are great ways to help keep the code organized. There are certain ways that you will be able to work with these in order to get them to execute inside of the code properly. In this chapter, we are going to spend some time talking about what strings and arrays are and how you would be able to work with them inside your code.

What are strings?

Inside of the Fortran code, all characters are going to be seen as one of two elements. They are seen as either single characters or contiguous strings. So what is the difference between them? With a contiguous string, you will notice that their length for syntax declaration is going to be passed, they will allow you to do notations on the substring, they won't allow you to do notation on arrays, they can contain descriptors if needed, and in some cases there are going to be hidden arguments inside.

When you want to declare a string inside of Fortran, you are going to use rules that are similar to declaring some of the other variables. So in order to do this, you would use the following option (we are giving the string an assignment of 10):

```
specifier :: variable_name

character(len=10)::name
```

Now in addition to working on the string, you will be able to work on substrings, which are basically just smaller parts of the string. They are going to be any part of the program that is executed and you are able to extract them if you wish. For example, if you have a long string that is several sentences long, you could work on a substring and just take out a few of the words to make it easier to read if you want. Here is an example of how you would be able to take out substrings from the string inside the code:

```
program string_concatenation
implicit non

        character (len=5) :: name
        character (len=50) :: announcement
        character (len=50) :: message

        name = 'Dana Caulfield'
        announcement = 'This is'
        message = 'I would like to give you a warm welcome to Prescott Academy!'

print *, announcement, name
print * , message
end program string_concatenation
```

With this option you are going to get the message "This is Dana Caulfield. I would like to give you a warm welcome to Prescott Academy!" You are able to choose how much of the message you would like to do and you can keep it all on one line or on more than one. For example, you could choose to just have "This is Dana Caulfield" show up on the screen if you would like. This gives you some options to have a longer phrase there if you would like while also keeping it so that you get smaller patches as well.

Concatenation

Another thing that we are going to take a look at when working inside of Fortran is known as concatenation. You are going to notice that it will use the (//) symbol in order to show that this is inside the code. The concatenation property is the one that describes which programs are able to link back to each other. Because of these connections that are established, the main goal is to either draw attention over to another branch in the program, or to make sure that the framework is solid. In some cases the links are going to be for two separate programs, but often the subjects are going to be single elements.

You can also work with a process that is known as trimming. This is when you want to cut out parts of the line that are not necessary so that you get the right result to show up. Since there can often be elements inside the program that aren't needed and are known as trailing blanks, the process of trimming is going to help to get rid of some of this clutter so that you are able to just use the portions that are needed. It also helps your compiler to be able to read through the code faster.

There are a lot of things that you are able to do with the strings inside of your projects and you will be able to mess around with them a bit to get the strings to work out the way that you want. But using concatenation and trimming will help to ensure that you are using the strings in the proper manner.

Arrays

Arrays are another important part of working on your code. They are going to be in charge of storing information, such as variables and characters, that are similar. If the piles of data aren't stored in the proper way, it is going to be really hard for the computer to be able to interpret them. However, when you use the arrays properly to put this information in the right places, the compiler is going to have a better chance at running the program and the functions will be executed in the proper way. Some of the things that you should remember about arrays to make it easier include:

- If you would like to specify the individual elements, you are going to need to address them using the subscripts. The first element is going to have the subscript of 1.
- If you see the term "extent' it is going to describe the elements that are along a dimension. Keep in mind that this is a numerical value.
- On the other hand, if you see the term rank, it is going to describe the dimensions that they have, using a numerical value as well.
- When you see the term "size" this is going to describe the elements that the array has, using numerical values again.
- The shape of the array is going to consist of elements.
- They are going to be declared with the attribute of dimension.

- They are going to be linked to memory locations that are contiguous.

There are two types of arrays that you are able to find inside of the Fortran language. The one-dimensional arrays are the ones that will serve as vectors while the two-dimensional arrays are the ones that will serve as the matrices.

Now that we know a little bit more about arrays, it is time to understand how you are going to be able to declare the arrays. Luckily this is a process that is pretty easy to complete. The rule is to specify the dimension that you desire, and then the compiler will be able to take a look at the elements that are involved and determine if they are an integer or real. For example, if you want to declare an array that is the Caulfield Lair and you want to give it seven elements, you would use the following code to make it happen:

```
real, dimension (7) :: Caulfield Lair.
```

Now you can also choose to declare an array that is two dimensional. Let's say that we are still using the example of Caulfield Lair from above, but we are going to make it so that the elements are 7 by 7. To do this, we are going to use the following syntax:

```
integer, dimension (7, 7) :: Caulfield Lair.
```

If you would like to make sure that you are assigning the right values to your arrays, you will find that the process is pretty simple. You just need to work on the array and then enter in the amount that you would like to use. You do have some choices when it comes to doing this because you can either do it on a single element that you want to change or you can work it out on the whole array. Let's take a look at an example of how this would work. Let's say that we want to add in the value of 3 to all of the elements would need the following code:

```
do I = 1, 7
        Caulfield Lair = i*3.0
```

end program do.

But on the other hand, if you would like to assign the value of 3 to just the first level of the array and then add different numbers to the other levels, you would need to use the following code to make it happen:

Caulfield Lair (1) = 3

Working with strings and arrays are a good way to make sure that you are getting the code to work in the right way. The strings are going to be statements that happen inside the code and make it easier for you to write out the different things that you would like to have happen, either by adding in the whole string to the code or just having a few parts as you see fit. The arrays are going to be responsible for holding large pieces of data in a way that is easier to look through and reach inside the code. Both of these are going to be important to ensuring that you get more out of the code and that it works the way that you want.

Chapter 4: Manipulating the Variable Amounts

Now at this point we are going to take some time to look at the different operators and variables that you are able to use inside of your code. So far at this point we have learned a bit about how to create a simple program. But there is a lot of manipulation that you are can do inside the code and operators are a great way to help you to do this. The operators inside of Fortran is going to be a great way to do mathematical functions while also getting these results to show up on the screen. With all that we have learned so far about this program, it is now possible to work on a short program on our own that will help to manipulate the amounts of variables. So basically inside of this chapter, we are going to learn how to make our program in Fortran do some basic math.

First we need to take a look at what the variable is all about. A variable is basically a little container that is going to store information inside of the memory of the computer. You are able to use these to hold either one or more value of your choice, and you are able to assign this either at the beginning of your block of code or when the code is being executed.

Assigning a variable is going to be pretty easy to accomplish. You will just need to use the (=) in order to pick the value that you would like to use along with the variable. You are able to add more than one value to the same variable if you would like to store them together in the code, but for the most part, it is just going to be one variable that you are working with. You can add in many different variables inside of the code, but the operators that we are going to talk about in a minute help to make it easier to get this all done.

Before we get too far into making this kind of program, we are going to take some time to work with operators. While these are pretty simple, there are some times when they can seem confusing and will make you wonder what they mean. The trick with these is to not think of them as mathematical symbols. For example, when it comes to writing out a = 2, you should see this as the value of 2 is going to be stored inside the memory of your computer that is labeled as a. Here is another example that you can use:

```
a = 2

b = 3
```

c = a + b

In the statement that we did above, you will see that the value of 2 is going to be stored as the memory location that is a and then you will see that the value of 3 is stored in the memory location that is called be. And then when you add the values of a and b together, you are going to store that result under the memory location of c. Keep in mind with this one that you are not able to write out this kind of equation as a + b = c because the compiler is going to see this as an error. The one variable needs to be on the left-hand side of your symbol and then you can have as many of the variables as you would like on the right-hand side, but mixing these around are going to cause an error message.

Arithmetic operators

Now that we have looked at some examples of operators, it is time to work with some of the operators that you need. Not all of the math symbols that you will need are going to show up on the keyboard, but the Fortran does have some of its own symbols that you are able to use in order to represent the different math operands that you are able to use. Some of the most common arithmetic operators that you are able to use on your language includes:

- (+): this is the one that you are going to use for addition
- (-): this is the one that you are going to use for subtraction in the code.
- (*): this is the one that you are going to use for multiplication
- (/): this is the one that you can use for division

One thing to note with these is that you can use more than one of the symbols, whether you are using three addition signs or an addition and a division symbol, inside the same part of code. You are able to use as many of these as you want, but you need to use the order of operands to do it. This means that you will need to do all of the multiplication, then the division, addition, and subtraction, going from left to right to make sure that the compiler is going to give you the right answer.

Other parts of your code

As a beginner, you will wonder what all the blanks, or the skip positions, are inside of the program. Some people choose to write out their programs without using these at all, but for the most part, the programmers like to include these inside of their code in order to make it easier to read. You are able to choose how you would like to use a skip position, but you should include at least a few to make sure that your code is easier to read through.

There are also some special characters that you are able to work with inside of your code. These are used in order to deliver the function that you want. These are going to seem pretty simple and plain but you need to be careful about how you use them. If you use them the wrong way or place two of them into the code right next to each other, you could end up with conditions that cancel each other. Some of the special characters that are found inside of Fortran and that you should watch out for include:

- (/): this one is going to specify another line
- (“): to output strings
- (:): this is going to terminate a list
- () this is going to categorize the descriptors.

Descriptors can be a tool that you are able to use and they are variables that are going to specify the amount of data that is required for a conversion. It is a good idea to keep track of the usage of these since the process may not end unless you add in the right descriptor is placed inside. Some of the descriptors that you can use include:

- A: repetition
- D: this one is for digits next to your decimal points.
- E: this is for an exponential number
- M: this is the minimum amount of digits.
- W: this is width in total characters.

You are going to be able to use all of these different parts to help you to get the code to work the way that you would like. You can mix and match a few of the parts to get the variable to be the right number, to store it in the right place inside the code and to do so much more. When you are able to add in the operators of the Fortran code, work with the blanks or the skip positions to make the code easier to use, and add in the special characters and the descriptors to the code, you are going to get a lot of power and options inside of the code.

Chapter 5: Working with Conditional Statements

At this point, we are going to take some time to look at the if statements. These are the most basic of the conditional statements and you will find that they are pretty straightforward. With this one, you will set the condition that needs to be met as well as the action that will show up at the same time with it. If the user puts in an input that matches, you will see that the program puts up the action that you choose. On the other hand, since this is a simple equation to work with, when the user puts in an input that is seen as false, the program is just going to end because you didn't set up an action.

So for this one, let's say that you just want people who are 18 to be able to get into the website. You would set up the if statement to accept any answer that is 18 and above. If the user places their age inside to be 20, the action (such a statement that you choose) will be executed by the compiler. But if the user puts in that their age is 16, then the program is going to see that this answer is false compared to the conditions that you set, and since you are using the if statement, nothing is going to happen.

Now there are some issues that can come up with this, but let's just focus on learning the syntax and getting this part down. Take a look at the syntax below for this:

```
if (x == 1) then

print *, 'turn left'

end if
```

The logical operator is the one that is used in this example along with the statement of if..then..end if. Note the expression that comes after the if statement. It is going to provide you with a test, something that is necessary when you are trying to imply a condition. In this case, we are going to assume that the "x" variable is an integer. One of the values that it can be is equal to 1. Interpreting this as a logical operation, the program is going to test to see if the value of the variable is 1. Then it will check if this is true or not. If your variable is 1, then the statements that come next will be executed which in this case would be the words "turn left". Then the end if is going to terminate the program that you are working on.

The if...else statements

As we mentioned in the last part, the if statement is going to be pretty basic and there are some issues with it. Your user may very well be 16 years old and it isn't a good idea to have the program just end if they put in this answer. You most likely will want to have some message come up at least, so that the user doesn't assume that something is wrong with the program. For example, if they put that their age is over 18, you would want to set it up to say something like "Welcome to the site!" and then have the next action be that they can get in. But if they put in that they are 16 or something else, you would rather have a message like "Only those over 18 are allowed in the game!" than having the program just end.

The if...else statement is able to help you to do that. You would set it up like the first part that we had above, but then you would add the else that catches anything that is considered false by the compiler based on the conditions that you set. This allows you to have an answer, any answer, come up regardless of what input the user is giving to you. This makes it much more clean cut and easier to deal with and doesn't leave the user wondering what is wrong with the user.

In addition, you are able to make it so that there are several options that come up. Let's say that you would like to have someone pick out their favorite color of either red, green, yellow, or blue. You would just need to write out more of the else sections of this code would just keep going. Another really useful thing for you to learn how to use inside of your Fortran code is the conditional statement. These are really great because they allow you to have some extra power and choices inside of the code. These will allow you to put in the conditions that need to be met in order to get different statements or actions to occur. They can be really simple, such as the if statement, where you will only have an action happen when the answer is inputted is true compared to your conditions, you can have it so that a different action will happen based on if the answer is true or false based on your condition, or you can give the user some choices.

You can decide what conditions need to be met before you allow the user to put in their information. This allows the code to keep things simple and it can look at your conditions before executing what you would like to have happen. You can make these as complex or as simple as you would like, but remember that you do need to base these on Boolean expressions. You have to leave the answer as either true or false based on the conditions that you set.

Don't worry if this sounds complicated right now. We are going to take some time to look over the different conditional statements that you are able to work with and help you to get the results that you want, no matter what kind of conditional statement you are working with.

The if statements

down the line, taking a look through each condition and statement that you put onto the screen. You can also add in a catch or break at the end so if the user picks pink or another color that isn't listed there so they still get an answer.

There are so many options that you are able to do with the if...else statements and they can really open up a lot of what you are able to do inside of your code. You can make them as simple or as complex as you would like, adding in more sections or just having a true and false option. Mess around with this a bit and see what you are able to come up with on your if...else statements.

Conclusion

Working in a coding language can be difficult no matter who you are. Many beginners are worried that they are not going to be able to find the answers to getting started or that it is just going to be too hard for them to pick out how to work with this code. But when it comes to working in Fortran, you will find that writing out a code can be nice and simple and it won't take that long for you to learn it and start working on your own.

This guidebook is going to take some time to help you learn how to work with the Fortran code. We are going to start out with writing some of our own codes while learning about some of the basics that come with Fortran. We will then move on to working with strings and arrays, understanding how the loops work, and even working with conditional statements. These are actually really important parts of working with a coding language, but since Fortran is so simple to work with that you will be able to add them into a code in no time.

When you are ready to get started on writing some of your own codes and want to get into the world of coding, working with Fortran is one of the best options to help you to get this all done. It is an older language that is meant for beginners and you will be able to catch on to it in no time at all. Use this guidebook to learn what you need to know in order to get the Fortran language to work for you.

Book 2
Hacking

By: PG WIZARD BOOKS

Top Online Handbook in Exploitation of Computer Hacking, Security, and Penetration Testing!

Hacking: Top Online Handbook in Exploitation of Computer Hacking, Security, and Penetration Testing!

Hacking: Top Online Handbook in Exploitation of Computer Hacking, Security, and Penetration Testing!

Table of Contents

Introduction

The world of hacking is an interesting world. Most of us only understand what is going on based on the movies that we watch or the news that we read about hackers stealing identities of those around them. These are parts of the whole hacking world, but there is so much more that comes with it. For example, some hackers are considered ethical hackers, which means that they are going to work to prevent others from getting onto their own systems, or the systems of others they are working for.

This guidebook is going to take some time to discuss the basics of the hacking world. We will start out with the difference between white hat hackers and black hat hackers and how each of them are going to work on the hacks that they are creating. We will then move on to working with how to map out your hack, especially if you want to check for vulnerabilities inside of your own system. And then the rest of the book will spend time looking at some of the common types of hacking that you can do including man in the middle hacks and even hacking passwords.

Even when it comes to hacking into a network that you are allowed to be on, it is important to learn how to do some basic hacks because you will be using the same methods that the black hat hackers are doing as well. This guidebook is going to help you to get started with doing some of the hacks that you need to ensure that you are getting the best results that you want.

Chapter 1: Some of the Basics of Computer Hacking

The process of hacking has gotten a bad name, mainly because of all the stories that have gone on in the media and in the movies about this topic. We may imagine someone who is just trying to get onto a system the are not allowed to be in or about someone who hacks into the government computers in order to get some important information and save the day. But there are many different facets that come up when we are talking about hacking and while some hackers are interested in stealing information and being places they aren't allowed to be, there are some who are more interested in learning hacking in order to protect their own computer systems and information.

There are two main types of computer hacking that you can come across. These include:

- Black hat hacking: this is the type that is found inside the movies. This is when someone tries to get onto a system that they don't belong, without the permission of the person who owns the system. Often this is done so that the hacker is able to get information they are not supposed to have, such as your personal information and credit card numbers.
- White hat hacking: this is the type of hacking that you may do when trying to keep your computer system and information safe from someone who may try to get the information and use it for their own reasons. Also, white hat hackers may also work with a big company, working on hacking on the system to see if it is vulnerable, in order to keep other people out of the system.

Both of these types of hackers are going to use the same methods to do the hacking, but the reasons behind the hacking are going to be completely different. It is important to note that black hat hacking is illegal and if you do this kind of hacking, it could end up with you going to jail and in a lot of trouble. But there is nothing wrong with hacking on to a system that you have permission to be on, such as your own personal computer, to help keep it safe or as part of your job.

Penetration testing

Now that we have a little basics of the world of hacking, it is time to look more into the world of computer hacking. We will start this out with penetration testing. This is known as an authorized attempt in order to exploit a computer system in the hopes of learning the flaws that are inside of it so that you can work to make it more secure. When you are given the assignment to do a penetration test, or you decide to do it on your own system, you will be investigating the system in order to prove that there are vulnerabilities in the network.

After you are done with doing the penetration test, the mitigation measures will be made in order to address any of the issues that you found and fix the issues that you discovered during this test. It is basically a process of finding the threats that are present inside of the system and then come up with a good plan that is going to take care of the issues that show up during the test. Doing these on occasion to the system can ensure that you catch the vulnerabilities inside the system before someone else gets on and steals your information.

Penetration testing is also known as ethical hacking. There is a very thin line that is present between vulnerability assessment and penetration testing. These terms are often interchanged but they are not really the same thing. For example, the vulnerability assessment is going to be responsible for evaluations the system for any security issues that may be present already. But the penetration test is going to be the test that is used in order to exploit and also proves that these security issues exist. The test is going to allow the hacker to test out the system as an outside source so that they can see how the vulnerabilities are affecting things.

As a white hat hacker, you would want to go through the system and perform the same actions that a black hat hacker would do on the system in this kind of test. You would try to get onto the system to see how bad the vulnerabilities are and to determine what information others are able to see. While the black hat hacker would simply do this in the hopes of trying to get onto the system and exploit it for their own personal gains, you are going to find out where these things are and learn how to close them up. Even though both of you will use the same methods in order to get onto the system, you are going to have different reasons for getting onto the system.

A hacking lab

As a beginner to working on hacking, you may want to consider working in a hacking lab. This is a safe environment that you are able to work in with the attacks and the traffic to see how they respond to different things that you are working on, without them getting out of hand and heading to places they are not supposed to be. This is a good place for a beginner to get started with because it allows you to get some practice without ruining anything in the system or causing some issues. Once you get a little bit more of the practice into the thing, you will be able to move out of the hacking lab and have some fun with hacking, and do some of the tests, on a real network.

While there are some differences in the reason for hacking between a white hat and a black hat hacker, both of these groups are going to use the same kinds of skills and techniques in order to get the information that they want. The trick here is for the white hat hacker to know just as much, of not more, and to be faster at finding the vulnerabilities compared to the black hat hacker. This will help to keep the system protected and ensures that the other group isn't able to get information they are not supposed to have.

Chapter 2: Mapping Out the Hack Before Beginning

So before we get too far in this process, it is important to come up with the plan that you want to use. This is meant to give you a good idea of what you need to do and where you want to look for some of these vulnerabilities inside of your system. The strategies that you will use are important, but you really need to focus on having a good plan in place before you get too far in this process.

When you are trying to find some of the vulnerabilities that are needed, you don't need to waste your time checking all of the protocols for security at the same time. This can make it a bit confusing and sometimes it is going to make you deal with more problems than you want because too much information is coming towards you. This means that you should break your system up into parts and then test each of these parts so that the work is more manageable overall.

For the most part, it is a good idea to start out with the application or system that you are worried about the most, and then go down the list until you get to each of them. To help you to determine which of the systems you should work with first, consider these questions:

- If the system is attacked, which system or application is going to cause the most issues. Which one has the most information or would be the hardest to fix up if it were lost.
- If the system is attacked, which application is going to be the easiest for the hacker to get in to.
- Which sections of the system are you working on and are considered the least documented, which means that they are rarely checked. Do you notice some that you have never seen there before?

As you answer these questions, it is going to become easier to figure out which applications you should work on first and it is easier to go through the whole process and find the results that you want. There are many places that you are able to check out to make sure the tests are run the proper way including the routers and the switches, workstations and laptops, operating systems, databases and applications, firewalls, files, and emails servers and more. It is possible that you will need to run many tests to get all of these so take your time and try them out to see where the vulnerabilities may lie.

When should I do my hack?

Once you have a good list of the applications and devices that you want to check, the next question that you may have is when is a good time to hack. You will need to make sure that you complete the hacks during a time that is going to cause the least amount of disruption in the company or on your own personal computer. This means during the peak hours of the day, you should not be doing these hacks because they could potentially cause a lot of slow down and issues with the system and depending on the type of hack that you do, and if it goes well or not, it could even shut down the network when it is needed most. The best time to complete the tasks is when there is going to be minimal disruption, so coming in after hours is often best since few people will be on the system or the building could be closed and no one will even notice.

The time that works the best for these hacks will vary depending on the situation. For example, if you are doing one of these hacks on your own computer, the timing may not matter as much because you would just pick a time when you are free to do the hacks and call it good. On the other hand, if you are doing this as a job for your employer, you will need to abide by their busy times and pick one that is not going to interfere with the business, especially if the hack does cause some issues.

Will others see what I am doing?

When you are working on these hacks in order to find some of the vulnerabilities that are in the system, you need to think just like a criminal hacker would, since these are the type of people that would try to get onto the system. Sometimes being able to look at the system through fresh eyes can make all the difference. For example, when you are used to using this system, you are an insider and could have troubles seeing what is going on in the system, but it is important that you make sure that when you do the hacks, no one else is able to see what you are doing. The criminal hacker would be careful about who is able to notice their presence so you would want to be the same way.

Now, it is your job to also check out what the hacker is able to see on your system. Hackers are always trying to find out as much information about the system as possible to make it easier to get onto it, and there are trails left all over the place for them to look at. As the ethical hacker of the system, it is your responsibility to find out what kind of information is out there for the other hackers to find and then learn how to diminish these trails to make your website and system harder to mess with. There are several different scanner types that you are able to use, such as a port scanner, so that you can see what information that is being shared, making it easier to catch some of these issues. Some of the other searches that you can do to protect your network includes doing a search online for the following information:

Any contact details. This is going to be information that can point back to the people connected with your business. Some options like USSearch and ChoicePoint are good ones to visit and see if your information is present there.

Look for any recent press releases that may talk about changes that have happened in the organization.

Look through any of the acquisitions and mergers of the company.

Always see if you can find any SEC documents about the company online.

Any patents or trademarks that are associated with this company.

Incorporation filings. These are also found through the SEC, but sometimes they are located elsewhere.

Be as thorough as possible about this point so that you have a good idea of what hackers are able to find out about your company or about your network. Often doing a keyword search is not going to bring up the results that you would like so you need to work with some advanced searches to find out all the information that you would like. At this point, you have a good idea of the different things that your computer or your network is sending out to other people and you can create the plan to get it all under control. Deleting information from online can help but running some port and network scans are great as well. Go through as many of these scans and tests as you can to help keep the computer network as safe as possible.

Chapter 3: Doing a Spoofing Attack

The first type of attack that we are going to explore is the spoofing attack. Whether you are working as a criminal hacker or as an ethical hacker, there are a lot of things that you can work with in order to get into a system that you shouldn't be on. As a hacker, you are responsible for researching and having some patience to wait in order to find the vulnerability that is on the system or network before taking the next move. But with the right kind of work, it is easier to get on the network and often a few different options are going to show up for you. One method that you can use is the spoofing technique that allows you to convince the computer system that you should be there so that you can get all the information that you want. Let's take a look at how this works and how you can make it happen with your hacking.

Spoofing

One of the first techniques that we are going to explore in this guidebook is spoofing. This is basically going to be a technique where the hacker is able to pretend that they are another person, software, website, or organization in order to convince the network that they are supposed to be here. The hacker is meant to look like this other person so that the network will allow them through the security protocols and then the hacker can get through where they want, get the information that is needed, and even leave the system before anyone else is able to see them. There are a few options that you are able to pick from when it comes to the spoofing technique including:

IP spoofing

With the technique of IP spoofing, the hacker is going to mask up their IP address or make changes to it so that the network things that the hacker belongs to the network. The hacker is able to make these changes so that the IP address either matches up with what is allowed on the network or it is one that the network is going to be familiar with. With this method, the hacker is able to be in any part of the world that they want, but the network is still going to allow them to get on because the IP address matches up in some manner. Once the hacker is able to get on to the system, they have the ability to take over this network, change files, delete things, and do some other tasks without ever being detected.

If the hacker is able to pull off this technique, it is very successful because it has convinced the network that the hacker is supposed to be there. The trusted IP address is found by the hacker and then it is used to get onto the network and make the changes that are needed. The hacker will be able to use this in order to gain full access to the whole system, whether they choose to sit around and wait for a good opportunity or they choose to do an attack and get the information they want right away.

DNS spoofing

Another spoofing technique is known as DNS spoofing. This method is going to trick a user who is trying to get onto a legitimate site. The hacker will take the IP address and then when a user clicks on it, they will be sent to a malicious website where the hacker has complete control. Sometimes the hacker will take over a legitimate website and turn it to their use, but often they will change around a letter or two to trick people. Users who aren't paying attention or who type in the address wrong will be sent to a bad website and the hacker can take credentials and private information from the user.

Often the user will not realize that they are being tricked. They will get onto the website and figure that it is just where they want to be. They can put in private information, send payment, and more while the hacker is collecting it all privately.

For the hacker to get this to work, they need to have the same LAN as their target. This requires the hacker to search for a weak password on one of the machines that is on the network, something that is possibly even from a different location. Once the hacker accomplishes this, they will be able to redirect all users to their website and easily monitor the activities that are done there.

Email spoofing

Email spoofing is one of the most common types of spoofing, which is one of the reasons that people should be very careful about the emails that they are receiving, sending, and clicking on. This can be a useful technique when the hacker wants to try and get past some of the security that is placed on email accounts. Most email servers are going to be good at recognizing if someone looks like they are legitimate and when something is spam, but there are also times when the hacker will be able to get past this and can send malicious attachments.

The most common form of this is when the hacker is able to pretend to be someone else inside the system so that they can intercept the emails from both parties, either read them or make changes, and then send the emails on without either of the two parties knowing. This can be really useful to the hacker because they can really get stuff done, and get ahold of private information that might be hidden elsewhere.

Phone number spoofing

When it comes to using phone number spoofing, the hacker is going to get ahold of some false numbers, or even area codes, so that they can mask their location. This is the best way for the hacker to be able to get into some of the voicemail messages that you have, and even to send out some text messages using this number. The target is often misled about where the hacker is from. Often this one is used when the hacker wants to pretend that they belong to a government office to trick the target.

The spoofing attacks can be difficult because often the network administrator is not even able to find out these attacks. The hacker will be able to stay on the network and cause almost as much damage as they want to these systems, without ever being found. It is often only after the hacker causes a big mess or when important information is leaked out that the hacker is finally caught and taken off the system. The hacker will be able to use just these kinds of hacks or some of the others in order to get the results they want and often they will be undetected by others on the same network.

Chapter 4: Man in the Middle Attacks

In addition to being able to do the spoofing attacks that we talked about in the previous chapter, it is also possible for a hacker to do a man in the middle attack. Sometimes the hacker will do this as a passive attack in order to just get on the system and see what information they are able to get, and other times they will use an active attack to get information, slow down the system, or cause some other form of problems.

When it comes to the man in the middle attacks, the hacker is able to do this with a form of spoofing that is called Address Resolution Protocol, or ARP. With this, the hacker is able to send messages that are false, but which are going to look normal, all over the network that they are working on. When it is pulled off, these fake messages allow the hacker to link up with another IP address of one of the users on the network. Once the hacker is done with this part, they can receive any of the data that all of the users are sending with this IP address and use it in the way that they would like.

So basically with this, the hacker is taking over an IP address and making it their own. They will receive all files, communication, and other information that is meant to go to the original user and they can use it however they would like. The hacker has the ability to get onto the network while receiving all traffic that goes on the network as well.

1. Session hijacking–this is when the hacker will use their false ARP to still the user's ID for the session. The hacker will be able to hold on to the information about the traffic and use it at a later date to get access to the account.

2. Denial of service attack–this is an attack done when the ARP spoof links several IP addresses to the target. During this attack, the data that should be sent to the other IP addresses are sent to one device. This is going to result in an overload of data.

3. Man in the middle attack–with this attack, the hacker is going to pretend that they are non-existent inside the network. Since they are hidden, they are able to modify and intercept messages that are sent between two or more users on the network. The one network may send a legitimate email, but the hacker will take it and change the information to be more

malicious before sending it on. The second user will open the malicious information, believing it to be safe.

Now that we know a bit more about a man in the middle attack, you are probably interested in learning some of the steps that are needed in order to complete the man in the middle attack. Here are some of the options that you can use and we are going to bring in the tool called Backtrack in order to get this done:

Do the research

The first step that you will need to do is find out the data that is needed to begin. The tool Wireshark is a good one to work with because it will help you to get all of this information to get on to the system. Firing up this tool on the network is going to allow the hacker to see what traffic is able to get onto the network through either the wireless or wired networks and is a really good place to get started for an access point.

Use your wireless adapter in monitor mode

Now that we have done some research, it is time to work with the wireless adapter and change it over to what is known as the monitor mode. This mode is going to make it easier for you to see the traffic that goes into your connection, even the traffic that isn't allowed to be there. This method is the one that you will work when using hubbed networks because you will find that the hubbed ones won't have as much security as you will find with the switched networks.

If you are able to see what information is going between the users that are on the switch, or you would like to make a bypass over this completely, you are able to work on making changes to the entries that are inside of your CAM table that is responsible for mapping out the IP and MAC addresses that are sending information to each other. When you are able to make changes to these entries, it is easier to get ahold of this traffic, make changes or at least read through it, and then send it back on without others knowing. The ARP spoofing attack is going to make this easier to accomplish.

Turning on backtrack

Now that you have changed the adapter and gotten it set up the way that you would like, it is time to fire up the Backtrack that you would like to use. You will need to pull up the Backtrack and then pull up all three terminals. Next, you will replace the MAC address from the target client with your personal MAC address. The code for doing this is: arpspoof [client IP] [server IP].

Once you do that, you will need to reverse the order of the IP addresses in the string that you just used. This is going to tell the server that your computer is the authorized one so that you are allowed to get onto the system and perform other tasks. You are basically going to become the server and the client so you can receive packets of information and change them how you wish. It also goes the other way around.

For those who are using Linux, you can use the built in feature known as ip_forward, which will make it easier to forward the packets you are receiving. Once you turn this feature on, you will be able to go back into Backtrack and forward these packets with the commandecho 1 >/proc/sys/net/ipv4/ip_forward.

This command is going to make it easier to be right between the client and the server. You will get all the information that goes between these two and as the hacker, you can use the information as you wish. You could look at the system, take personal information, or change anything you want about information that is shared.

Check out your traffic

At this point, you should be able to get access to all of the information that the users are all sending through the network. You will get to be right in the front row of this action and you can either watch the information that is being sent or grab ahold of some of it and make changes before sending it all back through the system again. You can use your BackTrack tool in order to sniff out the traffic and get a nice clear picture of the system. You need to take some time to activate this feature in order to make it work, but it can make things easier to work with.

Get your data as well as the credentials

Now you will just need to wait around and see when the client is logging into the server. Once the client logs on, you will be able to see their username and password coming up right in front of you. This means that the information is going to be right in front of you, making it easier to record and use it whenever you would like. Since the users and the administrators are all going to use these same credentials on all of the systems on the computer, you can keep using these credentials in order to get anywhere that you would like. You are now right in the middle of all the information on the system and you can use it in any manner that you would like, without other users on the system having any idea.

And now you are done creating your very first man in the middle attack. This is a great way for you to get in the middle of the all the action on a system, and the other users will have no idea that you are there. There are many things that you are able to do from here, such as intercepting information, changing the messages that are sent, slowing down the system, and even getting ahold of some classified information. this can really put the hacker right in the middle of the action so it is a great way for you to get started.

Chapter 5: How to Use Hacking to Get Passwords

The biggest target of hackers is to get passwords, mainly because they are really easy to get. Most people think that they just need to come up with a longer password in order to protect themselves, but there is more to it than that. If the hacker is able to use some of the tricks we stated earlier in this chapter, it does not matter how long your username and password is, they will still have it sent directly to them.

Confidential log in information, including passwords, are considered the weakest links in security because the only thing it relies on is secrecy. Once the secret is out, the security is pretty much gone. This is why it is such a big deal when a big company is hacked and all the username and passwords are leaked. The hacker is now able to get onto the system and use your information however they wish. Sometimes, the user themselves will inadvertently give out their own password for hackers to use.

So how do you hack a password? There are several ways that the hacker can do this including a physical attack, social engineering, and inference. There are also a few different tools that are used to crack passwords including:

1. Cain and Abel—this one is good to help with Windows RDP passwords, Cisco IOS hashes and more.
2. Elmcomsoft Distributed Password Recovery—this one is able to get PGP and Microsoft Office passwords and has been used in order to crack distributed passwords as well as recover up to 10,000 networked computers.
3. Elmcomsoft System Recovery—this has the ability to set administrative credentials, rest expirations on passwords, and reset passwords on Windows computers.
4. Ophcrack—this will use rainbow tables to crack passwords for Windows.
5. Pandora—this can be a good one to use to crack Novell Netware accounts either online or offline.

Some of these tools do have a shortfall because they will require the hacker to have physical access to the system they are hacking. But once the hacker has access to the system that you are protecting, they will be able to dig into all of your encrypted and password protected files with just a few tools.

Often, the hacker is not going to have access to your computer to do a password hack and they will rely on some other tools. Some examples of other methods used to hack a password include:

1. Dictionary attacks—these are attacks that will make use of dictionary words against the password database. This makes it easier to figure out if there is a weak password in the system.

2. Brute force attacks—these are capable of cracking all types of passwords because they are going to use all combinations of numbers, special characters, and letters until the device is cracked. The biggest flaw with this technique is that it can take a ton of time to uncover the password.

3. Rainbow attacks—these are good for cracking any hashed passwords. The tool is really fast compared to others, but it is not able to uncover passwords that are more than 14 characters.

4. Keystroke logging—this is one of the best techniques for cracking a password because it is asking the targeted computer to basically send over the information. The hacker is able to place a recording device on the targeted system to take in all the keystrokes done on the computer. The information is then sent over using programs such as KeyGhost.

5. Searching for weak storages—there are a lot of applications in computers that will store the passwords locally, making them vulnerable to a hacker. When you have physical access to the computer, it is easy to find the passwords through text searches and sometimes they are even stored on the application.

6. Grab the passwords remotely—often it is not possible to physically access a system, it is still possible to get the passwords from a remote location. You will need to do a spoofing attack first, exploit the SAM file and have the information sent to you.

Once the hacker has access to these passwords, it is easier for them to get the information that they want. They can use the passwords to get onto the network, to get to emails, find out financial accounts, and so much more. You must remember that passwords are a huge vulnerability in your system and to figure out more secure ways to protect your system.

Chapter 6: Getting Through Internet Connections for the Hack

If you would like to work on hacking online, you will need to learn how to get through the internet connection, as well as the security features, that are found online. Here we are going to talk about how to hack through a WEP connection as well as how to perform an evil twin hack so that you can check to see if your system is susceptible to this kind of attack or not:

How to hack a WEP connections

While there are a few different types of internet connections that you can work with in order to hack, this is one of the easiest to go through. If this is the one that your system is working with, you will definitely need to run through a few tests to see if you have been hacked or if you can make it more secure. Some of the things that you will need to check and hack through a WEP connection includes:

1. To get started, load up the BackTrack and the aircrack-ng. you can fire up BackTrack and then make sure that it is plugged into the wireless adapter to see if it is running. You can type in lwconfi in order to see if this is working. The program is then going to tell you which of the adapter it can recognize and if this is working properly, it is going to see yours.
2. Then take the wireless adapter and set it so it is at promiscuous mode. This will allow you to see what other connections are available and you can type in “airmon-ng start wlano” in order to do this. You can then change the name of your interface to have it read momo. You now have the adapter inside of monitor mode and you can type in “airodump-ng mono” to see which access points are available and what is attached to them.
3. Start capturing your access point. You will need to pick which connection you want to get on and then capture it. You can do this by using the command
    a. Airodump-ng –bssid [BSSID of target] -c [channel number] -w WEPcrack momo.
    b. Once you enter this command, the BackTrack is going to start capturing packets fro the access point on the right channel. This will

send the hacker all the packets that it needs in order to decode any passkeys that are present so they can get onto the wireless. However, it is important to realize that getting these packets will often take some time. If you need to get the packets quickly, it may be time to add in an ARP traffic.

4. Inject the ARP traffic—for anyone who doesn't want to wait around for the packets from WEPkey capture, doing an ARP packet and having it replay can help you get the packets that you need to crack the WEPkey. Since you already have the MAC and BSSID address from the target thanks to doing step 3, you will be able to use them to enter the following command:
    a. Aireplay-ng -3 -b [BSSID] – [MAC address] mono
    b. This will allow you to capture the ARPs through the access point of the target. You must keep going in order to capture the IVs that will come in as well.
5. Crack the WEPkey. Once you have the necessary amount of IVs in your WEPcrack file, it is time to run your aircrack-ng. Put in the command:
    a. Aircrack-ng [name of file]
    b. The aircrack-ng will enter the passkey in a hexadecimal format. You will just need to apply this key into your remote access point and then you are on the program. You can use it for free internet, to take over a computer on the system, and much more.

The Evil Twin Hack

The evil twin hack is an access point that will act like the access point that a user connects to, but it is manipulative. The target will just see their regular access point and think it is safe to get on, but this manipulative access point is used by a hacker to send the target to the hackers' premade access point, where the hacker can then start a dangerous man in the middle attack.

As a beginner hacker, you may need some practice doing the evil twin attack. Some basic steps to try out include:

1. Turn on BackTrack and start the program airmon-ng. Check to see if your wireless card is running properly by entering bt>iwconfig.
2. Once you have the wireless card, it is time to put it into monitor mode. You will be able to do this by entering the command bt >airmon-ng start wlano.
3. Now you need to fire up the airdump-ng. you will start capturing the wireless traffic that your wireless card is able to detect. To do this, enter

the command bt >airodump-ng mono. After this step, you will have the ability to see all access points that are in range and can pick out the one that belongs to your target.

4. You will need to wait for when the target connects. Once the target gets onto the access point, you can copy the BSSID and the MAC address that you want to hack into.

5. Now the hacker will need to create an access point that has the same credentials.

   a. First, pull up a new terminal and type in bt > airbase-ng -a [BSSID] –essid ["SSID of target] -c [channel number] mono

   b. This is going to create the access point that you want. It will look the same as the original access point so the target will click on it, but it puts the hacker right in the middle as the one in control.

6. De-authenticate the target—for the target to get onto your new access point, you will need to get them off the one they are connected to. Since many wireless connections will go with 802.11, everyone who is connected to the access point will be de-authenticated when you do this. When the target tries to get back on to the internet, they will connect automatically to the one with the strongest signal, which in this case will be your manipulated access point.

   a. To get the target off their access point, make sure to do the following command: bt > aireplay-ng –deauth 0 -a [BSSID of target]

7. Turn the signal of the evil twin up. The trick on this one is to get the fake access point to have a strong signal. It needs to be at least as strong, but preferably stronger, than the original point of access. This can be tricky because you are likely further away than the original access point.

   a. Iwconfig wlano txpower 27 will help you to turn up the signal on your access point.

   b. This can add 500 milliwatts to your power. If you are too far away though, this may not be enough. You either need to be closer to the target or consider a newer wireless card that is able to go up to 2000 milliwatts.

8. Put the evil twin to good use—once you have established the evil twin and you know that the target and the network are all connected to it, it is time to take the steps needed in order to detect all the activities going on in the system. It often depends on what you want to do with the system for where you will go from here.

a. There are a lot of options of what to do at this point. Hackers who have gone and created an evil twin are interested in more than just free wireless so they will often do man in the middle attacks, intercept traffic, add in new traffic, or steal information from the system, often without the target realizing.

Conclusion

Working in the world of hacking can be really interesting. There are a lot of people who are interested in knowing how to protect their own systems from a hacker getting on and finding out information that they shouldn't, but most of us assume that going through the process of hacking is going to be too difficult to get started. But with the help of this guidebook, we are going to be able to learn some of the basics of working in hacking and how to protect your own network easily.

Inside this guidebook, we spent some time talking about the different ways that you are able to work with hacking. We started with some of the basics of hacking, such as the differences between white hat hackers and the black hat hackers and discussed how they often use some of the same methods to get things done. In addition, we talked about working on mapping your attack so that you have a plan and how to work with spoofing, man in the middle attacks, password hacks, and even how to hack through different connections online. All of these can come together to help you understand how to do a good hack and keep things safe from a hacker.

It is important that you learn how to keep your information safe from others who will try to get on your network and steal it. This guidebook is going to teach you some more about hacking and how you can use it for your needs and to keep your computer system safe.

Book 3
Android Crash Course

By: PG WIZARD BOOKS

Step by Step Guide To Mastering Android Programming!

Android Crash Course: Step by Step Guide To Mastering Android Programming!

Android Crash Course: Step by Step Guide To Mastering Android Programming!

Table Of Contents

Android Crash Course: Step by Step Guide To Mastering Android Programming!

Introduction

Working with the Android operating system can be a great experience. Unlike some of the other coding languages and operating systems out there, Android is the language that you will work with for mobile devices rather than for your computer. With that being said, you are still able to work on the computer, using an emulator, so that you can check out if the app that you create is going to work properly or not.

If you are interested in creating some of your own apps with the help of the Android operating system, this is the guidebook that is going to help you to get it done. It is a simple program to learn how to use, and this guidebook is going to make it easier than ever to get started. We will talk about some of the basics of working with the Android operating system as well as how it is all set up for you to use. Once that is done, we are going to learn how to download the Android operating system, set up the emulator, write your first code, and even make some changes to it later on. There is so much that you are able to do with the help of this operating system and we are going to take a look at some of the best parts of it with this guidebook.

When you are ready to learn a new coding language for your mobile devices, and you want to be able to create some of your own applications, make sure to check out this guidebook for the basics on how to get started from doing updates, to installing the software and even creating some of your first programs.

Chapter 1: An Overview of Android

If you are someone who likes to work in programming and even on smartphones, then the Android operating system is a great option for you to use. Android is an operating system that is based off Linux, which makes it really easy for you to use. The user interface is considered as direct manipulation based and it is one that will be used and designed to work with tablets and smartphones that are touchscreens as well as cars, televisions, and wristwatches that are compatible with this technology. With the operating system, you are able to make use of the touch inputs which will be able to correspond with actions that are done in the real world, such as pinching, swiping, and tapping.

With all of the things that Android is able to work with, you are going to find many different projects that you are able to create. Android is a really low-cost operating system that is ready made and can be customized to the needs that you have. And since it is able to be used with other high-tech devices, it has become really popular with a wide range of technology companies. Add in that this is an open source operating system (which means that programmers are able to use it and make changes as they see fit), it is easy to use on your own projects, and you can even find a large community of developers who can help you out.

There are many features that you are going to find with the Android system. You will be able to use it with other languages to work on your device, it has the power that you need to compete with the Apple operating system and Windows 8.1 it is able to store all the information that you need, works with your Wi-Fi, and even has an interface that is intuitive for the user. These are some of the features that you can enjoy while using the Android operating system and with the new innovations that are always coming out thanks to this code being open sourced, you are sure to find other benefits that will help you to get your projects done.

Android is one of the best-operating systems out there for devices like tablets, televisions, and mobile phones. There are billions of these devices hooked up to the Android system, and it has quickly become one of the largest mobile platform bases with a huge growth potential in the future. In fact, according to the Google Corporation, it is believed that more than a million new devices are activated with Android each day.

The interface

By default, the user interface in Android is going to be base don the touch inputs of the user with options like pinching, swiping, and tapping on the objects, or the keyboard on the screen of the device. So basically this is an operating system that is designed to respond to the input of the user right away, and it includes a smooth touch interface to make things easier. You will also find that this operating system is going to put to use the vibration feature of the device, so the user is able to get some haptic feedback.

The internal hardware that comes with this operating system, such as accelerometers, gyroscopes, and proximity sensors are used by the applications, and you can use it for adjusting the orientation of the screen, using remote controls, and even change up the home screen for the different pages that you use. Basically, this is a very intuitive interface that the user is going to love because it responds to their touches and it has so many different options that they are able to use.

Managing the memory

For the most part, the devices that run on Android are going to use battery. So if you want to make sure that the battery life is going to last longer, you will want to have a RAM that will consume less power because they will not get a continuous source of power like some of your desktop devices. Whenever the app is minimized, or it isn't in use, it is going to be placed inside the memory automatically. Yes, these applications are going to be open still, but this method is going to help to prevent it from consuming all the resources of the system; they will simply wait in the background until you decide to call them back up.

This is great for the Android device because you will be able to call it back up as needed, but it helps to save the limited RAM that you have. The RAM is limited because you want to make sure that it doesn't waste out all the battery power that you have this device. Luckily, this system is going to be good at managing some of your applications. If it notices that your memory is running low, it is simply going to terminate the processes that aren't being used, closing up the oldest applications first to save room.

Security and privacy

Many people are worried about getting on a new operating system is whether it is going to keep your privacy safe and if it is secure enough to work on the apps with. There are many operating systems that promise to be amazing when it comes to your security and privacy, but some of them may fall short at some times and won't provide the benefits that you are looking for. But when it comes to the Android operating system, you are going to get all the benefits of a lot of security and privacy, simply by the way that the system is set up to deal with the work that you are doing and since you get to determine how all the apps interact on the computer and get to give each of them permission before they get any information, you know that your privacy is always going to be safe.

The applications that you use in Android are going to run inside the sandbox, which is basically an area of your system that is isolated and will not have access to the other resources unless you give permission for this when you install the application. Before you install a new application, you will also need to give permission in order to get it on the system. This is going to take a bit more time through the installation process, but it helps to prevent bugs in the applications, limits documentation, and helps to keep your information secure and private no matter what.

Works with different languages

One of the nice things about working with the Android operating system is that it is able to work with many other coding languages. Almost all of the major coding languages are supported on these devices, and the list is currently at over 100 languages. This makes it easy for the Android device to adapt to what you want to use. It also supports Java so that if you want to create something to work online, the Java language is going to be easy to use.

These are just some of the things that you are going to fall in love with when you get started on the Android platform. It is great to work with mobile devices, no matter what kind you have, it has a lot of speed and stability so that you know that your coding will work out well, and you can develop many different kinds of applications, in many different coding languages if you want, without too much hassle.

The benefits of working with the Android operating system

When it comes to working with an operating system that works out well with your mobile devices, none of them are going to be as great as the Android operating system. There are other options, but the Android operating system is going to work on billions of devices all over the world. Some of the benefits that you will be able to enjoy with this operating system include:

- Easy to use: working with the Android operating system can be really easy. You are going to learn how to create some of your own apps in no time, and then you can bring out your own creativity to work with Android or to create the apps that you dream about.
- Works well with mobile devices: the whole idea of using the Android operating system is so that you are able to use it to create apps that are good for your mobile devices. This can include things like televisions, tablets, and smartphones. You can use the emulator that is available for your computer, or your own device, in order to create an app and then have a chance to try it out to see if it works.
- Works with the Java language: you will need to know how to work with the Java language if you want to work on an Android app. This is a basic website and online building language that is easy to use, but it is important that you learn how to use this ahead of time.
- Allows you to create and sell your own apps: one of the reasons that a lot of people will choose to go with the Android operating system is because they have some ideas for apps that they want to use and hope to sell. There are millions of people who use the Android operating system on their devices, and they are always looking for new apps and games to work with. Some people choose to sell the apps for free, and others will make money off of the added space they sell or the cost of the app. This is a great way to make some extra money if you like to work with apps.
- The user interface is easy to work with: this user interface is meant to be really interactive. In fact, it is going to work mainly by the user working with their hands and fingers rather than relying on buttons and clicks like the other operating systems that you may be used to. This can make it

easier for you to learn how to make apps that the customer will love because they can work on it in real time without all the extras going on around it causing it to be slower.

- A big community to ask questions with: the Android system has a big community of people you are able to meet with, ask questions of, and so much more when you need help. Android has been around for a long time, and it has a lot of devices that will use this system to get things done. This makes it easier for you to use the operating system and to get it to work the way that you would like.

There are many options that you can choose when it comes to making a mobile operating system work for your app. Some people will use the Windows system and other times you will want to go with the Apple iOS. But none have the wide range and all the flexibility that you need from the Android operating system, and this is why so many people choose to go with it. With billions of devices that use this operating system and a million more being added each day, it is no wonder that people love being able to use and learn how to use Android.

Chapter 2: The Architecture of the Android Operating System

Before we get too far into developing our programs with the Android operating system, it is important to know some of the architecture that comes with this program and where things will work together. The framework of the application is easier to understand if we know how things are going to be arranged and will work inside of the operating systems. Since this is an operating system that is based on Linux, you will see that the two are very similar if you have worked with Linux in the past. For those who have never worked on Linux at all, you will notice that the layout of the language is pretty simple to use and you will catch on pretty quickly. Let's take a look at the architecture of this operating system.

Basic applications

The first applications that you are going to see are the basic ones. These are some of the options like the application to make calls, for your music player and camera and more. They don't have to come from Google, and sometimes Google isn't going to provide them at all, but you will be able to use the Google play store in order to develop these kinds of applications and make it so that they are available for everyone to use. You can also develop the apps with Java and then install them into the device that will integrate with the Android operating system.

Application framework

This is the part of the system that is going to be used for developing the applications. This framework is available with many different interfaces, and the developers will pick out which interface they want to use based on the standards that are important to them. By using these frameworks, you are going to save a lot of time and effort because it is not necessary to code out all of the tasks. There are also some different entities that come with the framework, and the options available are going to change based on the framework that you want to use.

Activity manager

When you are using the activity manager, you are using the part of the program that is responsible for managing the different activities that control the app life cycle. It is going to have many different states, and the activity manager will be able to handle all of these. The applications are going to consist of many different types of activities, and each of these activities is going to have its own life cycle. Whenever you launch up a new application, one main activity is going to be started. You will be able to pull up a window when needed in order to see every activity inside an app.

Resource managers

If you have some applications that are going to require some kind of external resources, such as an external string, these are going to be managed with the help of your resource manager. These parts are going to be able to allocate the resources in the way that is standard for your device and will make sure that everything works together well.

Libraries

There are several libraries that you are able to us in Android in order to make sure that you are using the right codes, to save time, and to make your work more powerful. All of the native libraries for Android are going to be found inside of this layer, but all of them are going to be written using either the C++ or the C language. The capabilities that are found inside these libraries are going to be similar to what you find in the application layer on the top of the Linux kernel. Some of the things that you are going to find inside of these libraries on Android will include:

- Surface manager: this is the compositing window in manager and display.
- System C libraries: these are the basic libraries of C that are going to be targeted for the ARM or embedded devices.

- A media framework: this could include options for playback, recording, video, audio, and more.
- OpenGL ES libraries: this is the one that is needed for the graphics on the device.
- SQLite: this is a database engine. This one, in particular, is a smaller version that works better on Android without using up as much memory space.

All of these are going to come together in order to help you to find out the codes that you would like to use inside your program. You can use these as a simple way to get started on the app that you would like to use or as some suggestions as to what you would need to do next. You can always add in some of the other parts that you would like if the code really needs it, but this is one of the best places to start as a beginner in order to get your basics down and to start writing some of your own code.

Android Runtime

You will find that the Dalvik Virtual Machine is the part that is in charge of the runtime for all Android devices. This is a virtual machine that is going to be used for your embedded devices as well as an interpreter for bytecode. They are going to have lower memories and can be a bit slower than you are used to since they run on batteries. You will find that the Java libraries are also going to be on these devices which means that you will be able to use them.

Kernel

When it comes to using the Android operating system, you will be using the Linux Kernel 2.6. This is going to include all the electronic equipment that you need, and many of the processes are going to be similar to what you will find with the Linux operating system to make things easier. Between the software and hardware of Android, you are going to see that the kernel will behave similar to the abstraction layer in the hardware and will include essential parts like the keypad, camera, and display. The kernel is also going to be in charge of handling things like the networking and device drivers.

Keep in mind that working with the Linux system means that everything is going to be in the form of a kernel. This helps to add in some security to the system and makes the whole program easier to use. If you have ever worked with the Linux system, you are used to how easy the Linux operating system is to do a lot of different tasks, and this is going to translate over to the work that you are doing over on the Android operating system as well.

Now that you know a bit more about the different parts that come with the Android operating system and how it does work quite well with the Linux system, it is time to move on to downloading this software properly and working on a few of your very first projects to make things easier.

Chapter 3: Working on Your First Project

Now that we have taken the time to learn more about the Android system, it is time to work on our first project. This one is going to be pretty simple to learn, but will help you to get a feel for how all of this works for some of the other topics we will bring up later on. But the first step that we need to take when getting started is to install the Android Studio.

To start with this, we need to see if the Java Development Kit, or the JDK, is installed on your computer or not. Some computers come with this already in place so that can save you time. For a PC, you need to click on Start, Run, type in the word "cmd" and then press enter to see if it is there. If you are on a Mac computer, you will use the Spotlight to search for the Terminal and then choose the top result. If this is on the computer, use the prompt "java-version." If a command is not found, you will need to visit the Oracle website and download the JDK on your computer.

Once this is done, it is time to go online and download the right version of the Android Studio for your computer. When this has had time to download the right way on the computer, you can click on Next to move on to the following screen. At this location, you will need to pick the setup that you want to use (standard is usually the best one) before clicking on Next and accepting the license agreements. At this point, the Android Studio is going to finish up the download, and you are ready.

For each version of Android that you are using, you will find that it contains a version of SDK for you to work with. The setup wizard is going to help you to get the updated versions of this. It is important to have the SDK because it helps you to set up the Android Virtual Device, the part that allows you to test your new apps on it and you can give it the right customizations for your own personal configuration.

So go back to the Welcome Screen of the Android Studio and click Configure. You should see a new menu that offers you a lot of options, and you will want to pick the one that says SDK Manager. A new window should appear when you click on this, and a series of folders, checkboxes, and statuses are going to show up. If you just downloaded the Android Studio, you should have the latest version of SDK Tools as well as some of the other tools to make the program work. If you see that an update is still available for this, the box will be ticked, and you can choose whether or not you want to take this.

Once you have had time to get the latest version of the SDK Manager on your computer (taking the time to update it if you need), it is time to create one of your first programs inside of the Android operating system.

Creating the OMG Android

Now it is time to start working on your very first project, and we are going to start out pretty simple, using the Hello, World! Kind of idea that the other coding languages go with. The idea behind this one is to give you some options and familiarity with using Android so that you can do some of the bigger projects later on.

The nice thing that you will notice about the Android Studio is that it comes with a nice tool that will give you the steps that you need to get this project started. You will just need to get on the Welcome Screen, click that you want to start a New Android Studio Project, and then the screen for project creation will show up. You are allowed to place an application name, and we are going to call this one OMG Android. For the company domain just put in your name. You may notice that the Package Name is going to change at this time to make a reverse domain name based on what you call the application and your company. This is going to be like a unique identifier so that the app is easily found among all the others.

Set the project location to the hard drive location that you would like before clicking on Next. On this screen, you are going to tell the system which devices and operating systems you would like to make the app work with. You probably don't want to make an app that will work with each Android device, but you can narrow this down to just smartphones or just tablets if you would like. For this one, to keep things easier, we are going to target the Android phone (you should see that this is the default option selected along with the Minimum SDK).

You can then click on Next to get to the following screen to choose what activity will happen for the app. A good way to think about this is as a window inside the app that will be able to show what content will be interactive with the user. You can use this activity as a popup or as the while window. Inside of this template, the activities are going to range from being blank with an Action Bar all the way to one that has an embedded Map View. But for this project, we are going to keep things simple and work with Blank Activity before clicking Next.

At this point, you are almost to the coding. We are going to go through and use the default options with this and then click on the Finish button. There will be a few minutes for the Studio to go through and finish off the project and sometimes you will notice that it is going through all the different steps and putting out information about what it is doing. The nice thing is that with this IDE, a lot of work is going to be done for you.

After a few minutes, the Studio is going to finish building up this project. This project so far is going to be empty since we didn't put in any code to it, but it will contain all the information that is needed to be launched on one of the Android devices. At this point, you should see that there are three windows that are open on the Android Studio. On the left is going to be the project folder, the middle will have a preview of what this looks like on the Nexus 5, and then the last window is going to show the layout of the project.

Right now the project is pretty empty and will not show much up on the screen, but you will be able to make changes to that later on and add in some words as well as some other really cool things. But for now, you have created a good program so let's take that a step further in the next chapter and not only add in some of the words or phrases that you need to work with inside this operating system, but also learn how to make the app run with your emulator or with the Android device.

Chapter 4: Running the App

So in the last chapter, we spent some time making a pretty basic app. We learned how to get it all setup and that the Android Studio is really great at setting the defaults that you want to use and which will ensure that you have it named the right way and ready to go. But so far the app doesn't have any words in it for others to see or any other actions, and it isn't running in a way that the other Android apps will be able to use. This chapter is going to take some time to add in these two options so that you can make your app start to work.

Running the app on an Emulator

So with the example that we did in the previous chapter, we took the time to create our first app, but now we need to figure out how to run that. If you already own an Android device, you are able to use this to run and test out the app, but if you don't have a device, you can choose to work with an emulator. The Android Studio is going to include the abilities that you need to set up a software-based device right on your computer. This basically means that you can run apps, debut the app, and look through a website on your computer, but it will work as if you were on the Android app. You will be able to set up as many emulators on your computer, and you can mess around with the screen size, version of the platform, and more to really see how the app is going to work.

If you went through the setup wizard properly on the last steps, you could already have the emulator in place on your computer. But we are going to take a moment to set up a brand new emulator in case you missed this option before or if you would like to choose a second emulator on the computer.

To get started on this is to click on the AVD Manager. You should be able to look inside of the toolbar for the icon that has the Android popping up and is beside a device with a purple display. The Android Studio is going to have one of these setups that you are able to use, and you will be able to see some details about the type of the emulator, the API that it uses, and the CPU instructions.

But if you would like to create a brand new AVD, you will just need to click on the Create Virtual Device. Now you will need to come up with some choices. For the first one, you will need to decide which device you would like to emulate. You should be able to look over to the left and see a list of categories that basically list all of the devices that you will be able to emulate and then you can see the different devices in each category. To make things simple, we are going to click on the Phone category and choose the Nexus S. once you pick this one, click on the Next.

Now you also need to decide on the Android version you would like to use. There are a few options that are available, and we are going to pick one of them, Lollipop. Check that when you are on this that the ABI column shows a value of x86 to ensure that the emulator is going to run at a good speed. Click on the Next button. This page should basically be a confirmation screen that you should double check before clicking on Finish and ending this process.

At this point, you have created a brand new virtual device that will allow you to test out your app. You should close down the AVD Manager and then head back to your main screen of the Android Studio. For the final step, you will click on Run before another window shows up and you can choose which device you want to test this app on. You shouldn't have any of the devices running here so you can start with the AVD that you created earlier, just make sure to click on the Launch Emulator and that the AVD is selected before clicking on OK.

Here you will need to give the emulator some time to load up, and you may even need to do this a few times to get it right. Once all of this is loaded properly, you will be able to see what there is of the running app.

So now that this emulator is all set up, it is time to add a bit more to the code that we did earlier so that we can see how it is going to work on other Android devices. We are going to keep this one simple right now, but you can always expand on this to get more out of it. So to start on this, you will need to go to res/values/strings.xml and then double click on this file. We are going to change this so that we can make it a bit more personal and have some fun with it. Here is the syntax of what you should type in:

```
<string name = "hello_world">I am learning Android!
```

```
</string>
```

You would be able to change up the code to say anything that you would like inside of this part of the code, making the string a lot longer, changing up the message, and so much more. This is just a great little way of showing how the code can work. But with this one, you have created your first app and even made some changes to make it a bit more personalized. You will just need to click on Run when it is done, and the message that you wrote out should show up on the screen.

Chapter 5: Doing Updates with the SDK Manager

Now we are going to take some time to do a bit more with the app that you want to create. This is all going to work regardless of the version of SDK that you would download on your computer so even if one of the older versions is there; it will still work. If you would like to make sure to open up the SDK Manager from inside the project, you will just need to click on the button that has the downward arrow with your Android peeking above it. When we are done with this section, we are going to be able to make a lot of changes to the app, and we will have one that has a PNG image, has an editable text field, and so much more.

So at this point, we need to have our "Hello, World!" app open and ready to go on the device, or you can use the emulator if that is the method that you would like to work with so that the message is showing. But now it is time to take this over to the next level.

Getting started on this project

For this one, we are going to take a moment to look ahead. The first thing that you will want to do with this step of the project is to make sure that the app is going to be simple. You don't want to add in a lot of complexities at this part because this can slow down the app, introduces some more bugs to the system, and just makes it more difficult for the user to work with. You only want to add in extra parts if you really need it for the app to work properly, but right now this is going to take some more time and work than what we want to work with at the time.

So to get started, we are going to need to open up the app/res/layout/activity_main.xml. If you are able to see the .raw and .xml file, you will be good to go. But if this is not showing up, you will need to go to the bottom of your screen and see if you need to switch all of this over to the Text mode. All we will do at this point is work to get rid of some of the attributes that are just padding to it. The Studio often adds these things to the .xml file on its own, but it can make it harder to work on the file. You are going to want to look for and delete all of these lines before we continue:

```
android:paddingLeft="@dimen/activity_horizontal_margin

android:paddingRight=@dimen/activity_horizontal_margin

android:paddingTop=@dimen/activity_vertical_margin

android:paddingBottom=@dimen/activity_vertical_margin
```

If you went through all of this and did it the proper way, your new .xml file is going to look like the following:

```
<RelativeLayout

xmlns:android=http://schemas.android.com/apk/res/android

xmlns:tools=http://schemas.android.com/tools

android:layout_width="match_parent"

android:layout_height="match_parent"

tools:context=".MainActivity">


<TextView

android:text="@string/hello_world

android:layout_width="wrap_content"

android:layout_height="wrap_content"/>


</RelativeLayout>
```

At this point, we will need to look for the Mainactivity.java part of the code. You will need to look on the left pane that is inside of Studio and then double click on it. We are going to take a moment to look at the very first piece of code, and you will need to move out a few of the lines including the following:

```
@Override
public boolean onOptionsItemSelected(MenuItem item){
//Handle action bar item clicks here. The action bar will
//automatically handle clicks on the Home/Up button, so long
//as you specify a parent activity in AndroidManifest.xml.
int id = item.getItemId();

//noinspection SimplifiableIfStatement
if (id == R.id.action_settings){
return true;
}

return super.onOptionsItemSelected(item);
}
```

You should be careful when you are doing this to make sure that you are leaving the final curly brace in its place when you delete the other options. This is the curly brace that is going to close up your class ahead of it, and you want to make sure that it is still there. Now that all the housekeeping work has been done, it is time to get to work and give the Activity a new life of its own.

Chapter 6: How to Publish Your Android App

Now that we have had some time to create our own app a little bit and learn how to manage the app in a way that makes it have less stuff in the way and so that it does more of the work that you want, it is time to learn how to publish your own app. You are going to work with making a lot of different types of apps over the years when you get familiar with working with the Android operating system and it is likely that you will at some point want to be able to publish one of the apps to make some money or for other people to be able to use it as well. In this chapter, we are going to spend some time learning how to take one of the apps that you create and getting it published.

The first thing to know is that when creating an Android app, you will need to publish it on the Google Play store. This means that you will need to create your own account using the Google Play Developer Console. This account is going to cost a little bit of money to create, about $25 at the publishing of this book, but considering the other parts of the operating system are free, this isn't so bad. The reason that there are fees with this account is that the Google company wants to keep out people who would make duplicate or fake accounts and helps to avoid people flooding the store with bad apps that no one else wants.

After you have gone through and created the account and paid the beginning fees, you are going to have your own Google Play Developer Account. You will be able to choose as many apps as you would like to publish on this account and you can choose whether you would like to publish those apps for free for others to use or in a manner to make money through the system. Some people are turned away by the fees, but if you are looking to make some money with this system on your apps by selling them, you will find that you can quickly make this $25 back. You can also allow ads to be on your app and earn some ad-revenue if you would like.

So to get this started, you just need to visit the site https://developer.android.com/distribute/index.html. Then you will just need to follow the steps that come up on the prompts to help you figure out what you are supposed to do to finish the account. In the end, you will finish creating your own developer account, pay the fees that are associated with the account to get it started, and then complete the process.

At this point, you are probably done with creating your append are ready to upload it into the system. You will just need to upload the app file in a manner that is similar to how you would attach a link or a document into your email. Then you will be asked to take a survey. This is not something that you will be able to skip out on because the system wants to know about the different factors and features about your app. Some of the questions that it is going to ask is about whether there are inappropriate contents inside and if there are any age restrictions on using the app.

After you are done with setting up your account and getting the app to upload inside of the program, you are going to need to give Google a few days in order to validate the app. You will be able to add in as many of these apps as you would like over time, but you still need to give it a few days before it is going to show up inside the app store.

And that is all that you would need to do in order to get the app to work inside of the Google Play Store. You will be able to choose to offer the game for free, add some ad revenue into the system to make money, or charge for people to use the app in the first place. There are many options about the type of apps that you are able to use, and since it is so easy to add it to the Google store, you will be able to develop the app, get it put up, and move on to the next project in no time.

Conclusion

The Android operating system is a great one for you to learn how to use whenever you are looking to create an app or another program that works on phones, tablets, televisions and other mobile options. It is based on the Linux system which makes it easy to learn how to use (especially if you already know how to use this system), and you will find that over 100 coding languages are recognized on Android, so you are able to pick the one that is best for you.

In this guidebook, we took some time to look at the different parts of the Android operating system. We started out with some of the basics of this system before moving on to how set up the architecture that is inside of the code, how to create one of your own programs, and even how to set up an emulator so that you can run the code on your computer (which can be nice if you don't have a specific Android device around) and see how it is going to work for you.

There is so much to love with the Android operating system. With billions of devices around the world using this system for making apps or running the programs that they want on their mobile devices, it is easy to learn how to use this operating system for developing your own apps or for your own personal use. Use this guidebook to learn more about how the Android operating system works and to make it create the best programs for you.

Book 4
Python Crash Course

By: PG WIZARD BOOKS

Step By Step Guide To Mastering Python Programming!

Python Crash Course: Step By Step Guide To Mastering Python Programming!

Python Crash Course: Step By Step Guide To Mastering Python Programming!

Table of Contents

Python Crash Course: Step By Step Guide To Mastering Python Programming!

Introduction

Learning a programming language can be a daunting task for many, but the right guidance can be the differentiator and the ultimate deciding factor as to how well you learn the language. Python is an easy to learn, high-level language which supports both structured and object-oriented programming.

This book aims at making the basic fundamentals of the language clear to the programmers. The dynamics of the language have been explained so as to enable developers to learn fine coding skills. Python has readable codes and an easy syntax thus making it simple to learn. It has automatic memory management system along with a comprehensive library that allows the programmers to write programs in a fewer lines of code as compared to other programming languages like C++ and Java.

Learning Python can be your stepping stone in the field of programming since Python methodologies can be used in a broad range of applications.

Lastly, the book is useful both for beginners who want to master this language and the experienced programmers who wish to revisit the basics or want a manual for reference.

We would like to thank you for downloading this book and we hope that the book is valuable for its readers.

Chapter 1: Preamble to Python

Python programming language was created by Guido Rossum in 1989. It is an object-oriented, multi-purpose and interactive scripting language. The language has been designed as highly readable. Python has fewer syntactical constructions and uses English keywords frequently. It is considered as a great language for beginners in the programming field.

Features of Python

1. Python provides rich data types and easier to read syntax as compared to other languages.
2. As compared to other programming languages it allows more run-time flexibility.
3. It is a platform independent scripted language with complete access to operating system API's.
4. Python libraries are cross-platform, thus making them compatible with Windows, MacIntosh and Linux.
5. It supports interactive mode that allows snippets of codes to be tested and debugged interactively.
6. It is a portable language and can run of various hardware platforms with same interface.
7. The Python source code can be easily maintained.
8. It provides support and an enhanced structure for big programs than shell scripting.
9. For building large applications, python can be assembled in to byte-code.
10. Python can be effortlessly incorporated with JAVA , C++, C , COBRA and Active X.
11. It can be used for programming video games, various scientific programs and artificial intelligence algorithms.
12. It has automatic memory management system.

Python is a self-sufficient language and consists of many tools and once the programmer becomes aware of their uses then it becomes an easy task for them. The language makes a solid foundation to branch out and learn other programming languages.

Installing and Setting Up Python

Python distribution is available for wide range of platforms. It is easy to install and nowadays many Linux and Unix distributions include the latest version of Python. To download and install Python you can visit http://www.python.org/downloads/ and opt for the desired version. Even though version 3 is the latest but still Python 2 is used widely. Once you have downloaded and installed you need to set up the path. To add the Python directory for a particular session in-

Linux /UNIX –

a) In the csh shell type setenv PATH "$PATH:/usr/local/bin/python" then press Enter.
b) For Linux, in the bash shell, type export ATH= "$PATH:/usr/local/bin/Python" then press Enter.
c) Type PATH="$PATH:/usr/local/bin/Python" in the sh or ksh shell and press Enter.
d) Please note that /usr/local/bin/Python is the path of the Python directory.

Windows-

a) Type path %path%;C:\Python at the command prompt and press Enter.
b) The path of Python directory is C:\Python

Running Python

There are three different ways to start Python. Python can be started from DOS, UNIX or any other system that gives you a shell window or a command-line interpreter. You can right away start coding in the interactive interpreter-

```
C: > python #Windows/ DOS
Or
python% #Unix/Linux
or
$python #Unix/Linux
```

A python script can be executed at command line by invoking the interpreter on your application.

IDE – Integrated Development Environment

You can run Python from GUI (Graphical User Interface) environment as well, provided you have a GUI application on your system that supports Python.

1. IDLE is the very first Unix IDE for Python.
2. For Python, PythonWin is the first Windows interface and is an IDE with a GUI.
3. From the main website the Macintosh version of python along with IDLE and IDE can be downloaded either as BinHex's files or MacBinary.

Make sure the Python environment is set up properly and is working fine so that you can execute your codes easily. (Python - Environment Setup)

Chapter 2: Basic Syntax

In the previous chapter, we learned how to install and set up Python. This chapter we will discuss the Python Syntax. A set of rules that defines how a program will be written and interpreted is called Syntax.

Let's understand various methods of programming

Interactive Mode Programming

At the command prompt type the below mentioned text and press Enter

print "Hello, Python!"

The output in version 2.4.3 will be *Hello,Python!*. Incase you are using the new version then you will have to use parenthesis along with the print statement–

print ("Goodmorning, Python!");

Script mode programming

The execution of script begins and continues till the script the finished upon invoking the interpreter with script parameter. As soon as the script finishes the interpreter will not be active any more. To understand it better take a look at this simple program.

Python files have extension **.py.** Type the source code *print "Hello, Python!"* in a test.pyf file and try to run the program as - *$ python test.py*. It will generate the following output –

Hello, Python!

Now presuming the availability of Python interpreter in /usr/bin directory, run the program as-

$ chmod +x test.py # to make the file executable

$ ./test.py

Output will be –

Hello, Python!

Identifies in Python

A name which is used to recognize a variable, class, function, module or other subject in Python is called as an identifier. An identifier begins with a to z or A to Z letters or a _ (underscore) which is followed more letters or a zero, digits (0 to 9) and underscores. No punctuation characters like %, $, @ are allowed within Python identifiers. It is a case dependent language.

a) Class names begin with uppercase letters and all other identifiers begin with a lowercase letter.
b) An identifier which begins with a single foremost underscore indicates that it is private.
c) An identifier with two leading underscore denotes a strongly private identifier.
d) The identifier is a language-defined special name in case it ends with two trailing underscores.

Reserved Words

There are certain reserved words in Python which cannot be used as variable or a constant or any other identifier name. All reserved words are in lowercase only.

not	exec	and
or	finally	assert
pass	for	break
print	from	class
raise	global	continue
return	if	def
try	import	del
while	in	elif
with	is	else
yield	lambda	except

Lines and Indentation

In Python, to indicate blocks of code for function and class definitions or flow control, there are no braces. The line indentation denotes the block of codes. In the indentation, the number of spaces is variable, but inside the block same amount of indentation should be done for all statements. Therefore, a block is formed by all the unbroken lines which have been indented with same number of spaces.

Multi-Line Statements

A new line in Python typically marks the end of a statement. However, the use of line continuation character (\) is allowed to denote the line should continue. Example –

```
Total = goods_one + \
    goods_two + \
```

goods_three + \

The line continuation character is not required for statements contained within brackets ( ), [ ] or { }.

Quotation

In python, all three quotes (' , " or """) are accepted. These indicate string literals provided the same kind of quote begins and closes the string. To cover the string across multiple lines, triple quotes are used.

Comments

The comment in Python begins with a hash (#) sign that is not within the string literal. After the hash all characters up to the end of the physical line form a part of the comment. However, they are ignored by the Python interpreter.

Blank lines

Blank lines are ignored by Python. These are the lines which have just whitespace, probably with a comment.

Multiple Statements on a Single line

On a single line multiple statements are allowed with a semicolon (;) provided that none of the statement starts a new code block.

Suites

In Python, a single code of block made by a cluster of statements is called as suites. The compound statements like if, else, while, def and class need a suite and a header line. The header lines start with statement (including keyword) and a colon denotes the end. They are trailed by one or more lines that make a suite.

Chapter 3: Python Fundamentals

Now that we know the syntax of Python, it is imperative for programmers to understand the python fundamentals. In other words, we would be discussing the basics on which the Python programming is based.

VARIABLES

A reserved memory location where values are stored is known as a variable. Memory space is allocated by the python interpreter and on the basis of data type of a variable it takes decision on what to store in this reserved memory. Hence, in the variables storing of characters, integers, or decimals is possible by assigning them different data types.

How to assign values to variables?

For assigning values to the variables you need to use the equal (=) sign. The left hand side operand denotes the variable name and the right side operand denotes the stored value inside the variable. Example –

```
counter = 10                    (integer assignment)
miles   = 100                   (floating point)
name    = "Tom"                 (string)

print counter
print miles
print names
```

In the above example-10, 100 and Tom are the values assigned to counter, miles and name variables respectively and will give us the result as –

10

100

Tom

Assigning a lone value to numerous variables at the same time is also possible.

Example –

x= y= z= 1

In the above example, with value 1, the integer object is created, and same memory location is assigned to all three variables. Apart from this multiple objects can also be assigned to several variables. Like –

x, y, z = 1, 2, "Tom"

Data types

There are many types of data which are reserved in memory such as; age of a person is defined in numbers, and his address is defined as alphanumeric. To define the operations possible there are several standard data types which are used**.** We are just writing a brief on them as of now and these will be explained in detail in next chapters .They are –

a) Numbers – As the name suggests numeric values are stored in this data type. Upon assigning a value to them number objects are created. Various numerical types that supported by Python are–
   (1) Signed integers (int) e.g. – 2, 4, 44 etc.
   (2) Long integers (long), they can be depicted in hexadecimal and octal as well. e.g.- 0122L, -0x19323L etc.
   (3) Floating point real values (float) e.g. – 5.0, 2.22, -88.88 etc.

(4) Complex numbers (complex) e.g. – 3e+26j, 45.j etc.

b) Strings –The adjoining set of characters depicted in quotation marks are called strings. Both single and double quotes are allowed in Python. The concatenation operator is represented as plus sign (+) and the repetition operator is represented as (*) asterisk.

c) Lists – These are mainly flexible data types in Python. The items in a list are separated by a comma and are written inside square brackets. The concatenation operator is represented as plus sign (+) and the repetition operator is represented as (*) asterisk.

d) Tuples - It is data type in sequence, similar to lists. A comma separates the number of values contained in tuples and unlike lists they are enclosed in parenthesis. Lists cannot be updated.

e) Dictionary – Dictionaries in Python are hash table types. They function like hashes or associative arrays and consist of key-value pairs. The dictionary keys are typically numbers or strings. The curly braces enclose the dictionaries and by using ([ ]) square brackets values can be accessed and assigned. For example, to create, add and delete entries in dictionary

```
# make a phone book:
phonebook = {'Tom Halter': 665544, \
'Liza Raymond': 889966, 'Ronald Johnson': 776655, \
'Kim Lee': 443344}


# add the person 'Mathew Peterson' to the phonebook:
phonebook ['Mathew Peterson'] = 99887766


del phonebook ['Kim Lee']
```

OPERATORS

The constructs which can manipulate the value of an operand are known as operators.

Python operators

1. Arithmetic

These operators execute various arithmetic calculations like addition, subtraction, division, multiplication, exponent, %modulus etc. For arithmetic calculation, there are various methods in Python like you can use the eval function, calculate and declare variable, or call functions.

Let us take a simple example –

a = 4

b = 5

print a + b

Output will be "9". Similarly other arithmetic operators like division (/), multiplication (*), exponent (**) etc. can be used.

2. Comparison

The comparison operator compares the value on either side of the operand to determine the relation between them. Various comparison operators are (!=, ==, >, <, <=, >=).

Example – we will compare the value of a to the value of b and print the result in true or false. Assume value of a =4 which is smaller than b =5.

Now when we print the value as a >b, it actually compares the value of a to b and since it is incorrect, it returns as false. Similarly you can use other comparison operators.

3. Assignment

To assign the value of the right operand to the left operand, we use assignment operators.They are (+, +=, -=, /=, *=, %=, **=, //=). Example-

num1 = 4

num2 =5

print ("Line1 – Value of num1:" , num1)

print ("Line2 – Value of num2:", num2)

Output –

('Line1 –Value of num1:',4)

('Line2 – value of num2:', 5

4. Logical

These operators are used for conditional statements which are true or false.

AND, OR and NOT are the logical operators in Python

AND – it returns TRUE if both left and right operands are true.

OR – it returns FALSE if either of the operand is true.

NOT – it returns TRUE if operand is false

Example-

```
x = true

y = false

print ('x and y is', x and y)

print ('x or y is', x or y)

print ('not x is', not x)
```

The result will be –

```
('x and y is', False)

('x or y is', True)

('not x is', False)
```

5. Membership

Inside a sequence such as strings, lists or tuples membership is checked by these operators. These are of two types (in and not in). These operators give result based on the variable present in specified string or sequence.

Example –

We will check whether value of x=3 and y=7 is available in list or not by using membership operators.

```
x= 3

y =7

list = [1, 2, 3, 4, 5];

if ( x in list):

   print "Line 1 – x is available in the given list"
```

```
else:
    print "Line 1 – x is not available in the given list"

if ( y not in list):
    print "Line 2 – y is not available in the given list"
else:
    print "Line 2- y is available in the given list"
```

Result of the above code –

Line 1 – x is available in the given list

Line 2 – y is not available in the given list

6. **Identity**

Memory locations of two objects are compared by identity operators. They are of two types – is and is not.

is – it returns true if two variables point the same object otherwise false.

is not- it returns false if two variables point the same object, otherwise true.

Example –

```
x = 10
y = 10

if (x is y):
```

```
        print "x & y SAME identity"

y = 20

if (x is not y):

        print "x & y have DIFFERENT identity"
```

Following result is generated –

```
x&y SAME identity
x & y DIFFERENT identity
```

7. **Bitwise**

   A bitwise operator work on bits and performs bit by bit operation. Python supports the following Bitwise operators - & Binary AND, | Binary OR, ^ Binary XOR, ~Binary Ones Complement, << Binary Left shift and >> Binary Right shift.

Operators Precedence

It determines which operator needs to be evaluated first. Precedence of operators is necessary to avoid ambiguity in values. For example – multiplication has a higher precedence than addition. Following operators are usedin Python – (**, ~+ -, */ % //, + -, & , ^|, >><<, &, <=<>>=, <> == !=, is is not, in not in , not or and)

STATEMENTS

Anticipating the conditions that might occur while executing a program and specifying the actions according to those conditions is called decision making. The decision structures assess numerous expressions which produce TRUE or FALSE as a result. You need to determine which action to take and what statements to execute if the result is TRUE or FALSE otherwise. In Python programming any non-zero and non-null values are assumed as TRUE, and if it is either null or zero then it is assumed as FALSE value.

Following types of decision making statements are provided in Python –

1. **if statements** - it contains a Boolean expression followed by one or more statements.
   A logical expression is used to compare the data and decision is made on the basis of comparison result. If Boolean expression evaluates to TRUE, then the block of statement(s) inside the *if* statement is executed. In case it evaluates FALSE, then the first set of code after the end of *if* statement is executed.

   Syntax –

   if expression:

   statement(s)

2. **if....else statements** – In this an *if* statement is followed by an optional *else* statement.If the conditional expression in the *if* statement resolves to FALSE value or 0, the block of code executes in an else statement.

   Syntax –

   if expression:

   statement(s)

   else:

   statement(s)

3. **elif statement** – It permits you to examine multiple expressions for TRUE and carry out a block of code as soon as one of the condition evaluates to TRUE. They are also optional statements and random number of *elif* statements following an *if* can be there.

   Syntax –

   if expression 1:

   statement(s)

   if expression 2:

   statement(s)

   elif expression3:

   statement(s)

   else:

   statement(s)

4. **nested statements** – When you want to examine a different condition when a condition works out to be true then you can use *nested if* statements. Inside a nested if statement, an *if...elif ... else* inside another *if...elif..else* construct is also possible.

   Syntax –

   if expression1:

   statement(s)

   if expression2:

   Statement(s)

   elif expression3:

   statement(s)

```
    else:
        statement(s)
elif expression4:
        statement(s)
else:
        statement(s)
```

Chapter 4: Learn about Python loops, Strings, Lists, Tuples, and Dictionary

We have already introduced these terms in the previous chapter. Now we will take a look at each one of them in detail so that you can understand their usage in Python programming.

LOOPS

Typically the statements are executed in sequence, but if a situation arises when you are required to execute a block of code many number of times. In Python, a loop statement permits you to execute a statement or a group of statements numerous times. To handle the looping requirement following types of loops are available in Python –

1. **while loop** – this loop repetitively executes a target statement as long as the condition given is true.
   Syntax-

   while expression:

       statement(s)

   Here, it can be a single statement or a block of statements and the condition may be an expression. The loop iterates as long while the condition is true. When the condition becomes false, the program control passes to the line immediately following the loop.

2. **for loop** – these loops have the capability to iterate over items of whichever sequence, like a string or list.
   Syntax-

   ```
   for iterating_var in sequence:
       statement(s)
   ```

The sequence which contains an expression is evaluated first and then the first item in a sequence is assigned to the *iterating_var*. After this the statement block is executed. All the items in the list are assigned to *iterating_var*, and the statement(s) block is executed until the entire sequence is exhausted.

3. **Infinite loop**– If a condition never becomes FALSE it becomes an infinite loop. The results in a loop that never ends are called as infinite loops. These loops might be useful in client/server programming where server needs to run continuously for the client programs to communicate with it as and when required.

Using else statements with loops

If an else statement is used with for loop, then the else statement is executed when the loop has exhausted iterating the list. When else is used with a while loop, the else statement is executed when the condition becomes false.

Loop Control Statements

The execution from normal sequence is changed with loop control statements. So when execution leaves a scope, all automatic objects that were created in that scope are destroyed. Listed below are the control statements that are supported by Python –

a) **Break statement** – it ends the current loop statement and transfers execution to the statement immediately following the loop. The break statement can be used in both *for* and *while* loops. Most common use of break statement is when some external condition is triggered requiring a quick exit from loop.
   Syntax-

   break

b) **Continue statement** – The control is returned to the beginning of the while loop. The continue statements reject all the remaining statements in the current iteration of the loop and moves the control back to the top of the loop. It can be used for both *for* and *while* loops.
Syntax-

continue

c) **Pass statement** – When a statement is required syntactically but you do not want any command or code to execute, we use pass statement. It is a *null* operation and nothing happens on execution.
Syntax –

pass

STRINGS

In python, strings can be created by simply enclosing characters in quotes. The single quotes are treated same as double quotes. It is as easy as assigning value to a variable. Python has a built-in string called as 'str' which has many features. A literal in string can expand into multiple lines but there has to be back slash at the end of each line before the new line is created.

Example –

var 1 = 'Goodmorning World!'

var 2 = ' Python Programming'

How to access values in strings?

A character type is not supported by Python, they are considered as strings of length one, therefore also considered as substring. In order to access substring, the square brackets are used for slicing along with the index or indices.

Example –

var 1 = 'Goodmorning World!'

var 2 = "Python Programming"

print "var1[0]:", var1[0]

print "var2[1:5]:", var2[1:5]

result –

var1[0]: G

var2[1:5]: ytho

Updating Strings

Existing strings can be updated by (re)assigning a variable to another string. The new value can be related to a completely different string altogether or to its previous value.

String operators

There are various string operators, assume variable **a** holds 'Hello' and **b** holds 'World'

Operator	**Description**	**Example**
*	Repetition –it prints the character twice.	a*2 will give HelloHello

+	Concatenation- adds value on both sides and gives results	a + b will give Hello World
[:]	Range slice – gives characters from given range.	a[1:4] will give ell
[ ]	Slice – gives characters from given index	a[1]will give e
not in	Membership – if a character does not exist in a given string it returns true	M not in a will give 1
in	Membership – if character exists in the given string it returns true	H in a will give 1
r/R	Raw string- it surpasses actual meaning of escape characters	Print r'\n' prints \n and print R'\n' prints \n
%	Format – does string formatting	Read below

String formatting

The string formatting % operator is exclusive to strings and makes up for the bunch of having functions from C's printf family.

Example –

print "My name is %s and weight is %d kg!" % ('Alex', 25)

Result –

My name is Alex and weight is 25kg!

Triple Quotes

A triple quote in Python allows the strings to span in multiple lines which include verbatim TABs, NEWLINEs, and many other special characters. The syntax for triple quotes include three consecutive double or single quotes.

Changing lower and upper case

In Python, you can change the string to upper case from lower case

str = "this is an example";

print "str.capitalize( ):", str.upper( )

Result –

str.capitalize( ): THIS IS AN EXAMPLE

LISTS

In Python, the fundamental data structure is a sequence. All the elements in a sequence are assigned a number; its index or position. In python, there are six built-in types of sequences and most common are tuples and lists.

Lists are the most flexible data type which can be written as a list of values separated by comma between the square brackets. The items in the list may not be of same type.

Example –

list 1 = ['english', 'french', 1996, 2015];

list2 = [1, 2, 3, 4, 5];

list3 = ["x", "y", "z"]

Just like string indices, list indices also start at 0, and list can be concatenated, sliced and so on.

How to access values in lists?

The square brackets are used for slicing along with the indices or index to get a value at the index.

list 1 = ['english', 'french', 1996, 2015];

list2 = [1, 2, 3, 4, 5, 6, 7];

print "list1[0]:", list1[0]

print "list2[1:5]:", list2[1:5]

Result –

list1[0]: English

list2[1:5]: [2, 3, 4, 5]

Updating Lists

Multiple elements or a single element of lists can be updated by giving the slice on the left-hand side of the assignment operator. It is possible to add elements in a list by using the append( ) method.

Example –

list = ['english', 'french', 1996, 2015];

print "Value available at index 2:"

print list[2]

list[2] = 2016;

print "New value available at index 2:"

print list[2]

Result –

Value available at index 2:

1996

New value available at index 2:

2016

Deleting elements from list

By using either the remove( ) method if you don't know which element to delete or del statement if you know exactly which element(s) you are deleting you can delete a list element.

Example –

list = ['english', 'french', 1996, 2015];

print list1

del list1[2];

print "After deleting value at index 2:"

print list 1

Result-

['english', 'french', 1996, 2015]

After deleting value at index 2:

['english', 'french', 2015]

Similar to Strings, lists also react to * and + operators; they mean repetition and concatenation here as well, except that the outcome is a new list, not a string. As the lists are sequences, slicing and indexing also works in a similar manner as in strings.

Python has some built-in list functions –

1. cmp(list1, list2) – it compares elements in each list
2. max(list) - it returns item from the list with maximum value.
3. len(list) – it gives total strength of the list.
4. min(list)- it returns items from the list with minimum value.
5. List(seq) – it converts tuple into list.

List methods –

1. list.append(obj)- it appends object obj to list
2. list.extend(seq) – it appends the contents of seq to list
3. list.count(obj) – it returns count of how many times obj occurs in list.
4. list.insert(index,obj) – it inserts obj into list at offset index.
5. list.index(obj)- it returns the lowest index in the list that obj appears.
6. list.remove(obj) – it removes object from list
7. list.pop(obj=list[-1])- it removes and returns the last obj from list.
8. list.sort([func]) – sorts objects of list, use compare function if given
9. list.reverse( )- it reverses object of list in place.

TUPLES

The series of unchangeable Python objects are called as tuples. They are sequences similar to lists. Unlike lists, you cannot change tuples and they make use of parentheses, on the other hand square brackets are used in lists. You can create tuples by simply separating values with a comma and optionally these values which are separated by comma can be put inside parentheses.

Example –

tup1 = ('english', 'french', 1996, 2015);

tup2 = (1, 2, 3, 4, 5);

tup3= "x", "y", "z";

Two parentheses consisting of nothing; *tup= ( );* denotes an empty tuple.

In order to write tuple that contains single value a comma needs to be included, even though there is barely a single value; *tup1= (45,);*

How to access values in Tuples?

Make use of the square brackets for slicing, besides the index or indices to get the value available at the index.

Example –

tup1 = ('english', 'french', 1996, 2015);

tup2 = (1, 2, 3, 4, 5, 6, 7);

print "tup1[0]:", tup1[0]

print "tup2[1:5]:", tup2[1:5]

result –

tup1[0]: English

tup2[1:5]: [2, 3, 4, 5]

How to update tuples?

Since tuples are unchangeable you cannot change or update the tuple elements values. You can take parts of existing tuple to make new tuples.

Example –

Tup1 = (14, 32.44);

Tup2 = ('xyz', 'abc');

#Below action is not valid for tuples

#tup1[0] =100;

Therefore let's create a new tuple

tup3 = tup1 + tup2;

print tup3

result –

(14, 32.44, 'xyz', 'abc')

Deleting elements in tuples

Individual elements of tuples cannot be removed. However, there is nothing wrong in positioning together one more tuple with the undesired elements discarded. In order to completely remove a tuple, just add **del** statement.

Example –

tup = ('english', 'french', 1996, 2015);

print tup

del tup;

print "After deleting tup:"

print tup

Result –

('english', 'french', 1996, 2015)

After deleting tup:

Traceback (most recent call last):

file "test.py", line 9, in <module>

print tup;

NameError: name 'tup' is not defined

Please note that an exception is raised because after del tup tuple does not exist.

Similar to strings, tuples react to * and + operators; they denote repetition and concatenation here too, but a new tuple is created as a result and not a string. The indexing and slicing in tuples works in a similar way as it works in strings.

Following are the built-in functions of tuples –

1. cmp(tuple1, tuple2) – it compares the elements in each tuple
2. max(tuple) – it returns item from the tuple with maximum value.
3. len(tuple) – it gives the total length of the tuple.
4. tuple(seq)- it converts a list into a tuple.
5. min(tuple) – it returns item from the tuple with minimum value.

PYTHON DICTIONARY

Dictionary values can be of any kind, but the keys must be of an unchangeable data type such as numbers, strings and tuples.

How to access values in Dictionary?

By using the square brackets along with the key to obtain its value dictionary elements can be accessed.

Example –

dict = {'Name': 'Tom', 'Age': 10, 'Class': 'Fifth'}

print "dict['Name']:", dict['Name']

print "dict['Age']:", dict['Age']

Result –

dict['Name']: Tom

dict['Age']: 10

Properties of Dictionary Keys

a) Per key you cannot have more than one entry, i.e. duplicate key is not allowed. The preceding assignment wins when a duplicate key is encountered.
b) Keys should be unchangeable. By this it means that you may utilize numbers, strings or tuples as dictionary keys but something like ['key'] is not allowed.

Built-in dictionary functions-

1. cmp(dict1,dict2) – compares elements in both
2. str(dict)- produces a printable string
3. len(dict) – gives total length of dictionary
4. type(variable) – returns the type of passed variable.

Built-in dictionary methods-

1. dict.clear( ) – removes all elements of dictionary

2. dict.fromkeys( )- creates a new dictionary with keys from seq and values set to value
3. dic.copy( ) – returns a shallow copy of dictionary
4. dict.get(key, default=None) – returns value or default if key not in dictionary.
5. dict.has_key(key) – returns true if key in dictionary*dict*, otherwise false
6. dict.keys( )- returns list of dictionary dict's keys
7. dict.items( ) – returns a list of *dict's* tuple pairs
8. dict.setfedault(key,default=None) – similar to get, but will set dict[key]= default if *key* is not already in dict.
9. dict.values( )- returns list of dictionary *dict's* values.
10. dict.update( )- adds dictionary *dict2's* key-values pair to *dict*

Chapter 5: Insight into Python Functions, Modules and Classes

FUNCTIONS

A block of code that is organized, reusable, and is used to carry out a single, related action is called as a function. The functions provide better modularity for your application and a high degree of code reusing. Python has many built-in functions but creating your own functions is also possible and these are called as *user-defined* functions.

How to define a Function?

In order to give the necessary functionality you can define a function. Here, are some simple rules for defining a function in Python –

1. A function block begins with the keyword def followed by the function name and parentheses (( )).
2. Any arguments or input parameters must be positioned within these parentheses. Parameters can also be defined within these parentheses.
3. Inside every function the block of code starts with a colon and is indented.
4. The statement return [expression] exits a function, optionally passing back an expression to the caller. The return statement with no arguments is the same as return None.
5. The first statement of a function can be an optional statement; the documentation string of the function or *docstring*.

Syntax –

deffunctionname (parameters):

"function_doctsring"

function_suite

return [expression]

Parameters, by default have a positional behavior and you need to inform them in the similar order as they were defined.

How to call a function?

By defining a function you only give a name to a function, structures the block of code and specify the parameters that are to be included in the function. Once the basic structure of a function is finalized, you can execute it by calling it from the Python prompt directly or from another function.

Example of function printme( ) is as below –

```
# Function definition is here
def printme(str):
   "This prints a passed string into this function"
   print str
   return;

# Call the printme function now
printme ("This is first call to user defined function!")
printme ("This is second call to the same function")
```

Output –

This is first call to user defined function!

This is second call to the same function

In Python, all parameters (arguments) are passed by reference. This means what a parameter refers to inside a function, if you change it, the change gets reflected back in the calling function.

Function Arguments

By using following types of arguments you can call a function –

a) Required arguments –these are the arguments passed to a function in correct positional order. In this the number of arguments in the function call should exactly match with the function definition.
b) Keyword arguments – These are related to function calls. Once keyword argument is used in a function call, the parameter name identifies the arguments to the caller. This allows for skipping of arguments or places them out of order since the keywords given to match the values with parameters is used by the Python interpreter.
c) Default arguments –in the function call if a value is not provided for the argument this argument assumes a default value.
d) Variable-length arguments – While defining a function it may be required to process a function for additional arguments than specified, these are called as variable-length arguments. Unlike default and required arguments, they are not named in the function definition. The variable name that carries the value of all non-keyword variable arguments an asterisk is placed before it. Tuple will remain empty in case there are no extra arguments specified during a function call.

Scope of Variables

In a program, all variables may not be accessible at all locations. This depends on where you have declared a variable. The portion of the program where you can access a particular identifier is determined by the scope of variables. There are two basic scopes –

a) Global – Variables that are defined outside the function body have a global scope. These can be accessed throughout the program body by all functions.
b) Local – Variables that are defined inside the function body have a local scope. These can be accessed only inside a function in which they are declared.

MODULES

Modules help in organizing the code logically. The code becomes easy to use and understand by grouping the related code into module. A Python object with arbitrarily named attributes that can bind and reference is called module. In simple words, module is a file that consists of Python code. It can define variables, functions, and classes.

Example of simple module support.py -

```
def print_func( par ):
    print " Hi:", par
    return
```

Import Statememt

Any Python source file can be used as a module by executing an import statement in some other Python source file.

Syntax –

import module1[, module2[,. . .moduleN]

From import statement

Specific attributes can be imported from a module into the current namespace with the help of *from import* statements.

Syntax –

from modname import name1[, name2[,. . .nameN]]

From...import * statement

The *from..import*statement* makes the import of all names possible from a module into the current namespace.

*from modname import**

Locating Modules

The module is searched by the Python interpreter in the below mentioned sequence when a module is imported.

a) Current directory
b) In case the module isn't found, the Python looks into every directory in the shell variable PYTHONPATH
c) The default path is checked in Python, if else fails.

The module search path is stored in the system module sys as the **sys.path**variable. This variable contains the current directory, PYTHONPATH, and the installation dependent default.

PYTHONPATH – it is an environment variable, which consists of a list of directories.

Syntax-

For windows -

set PYTHONPATH=c:\python20\lib;

For UNIX-

set PYTHONPATH=/usr/local/lib/python

Namespaces and scoping

A namespace is a dictionary of variable names (keys) and their corresponding objects (values)

Variable can be accessed in Python in both local and global namespace. In case a global and local variable has the same name, the global variable is overshadowed by the local variable. All functions have their own local namespace. The same scoping rules are followed by classes as ordinary functions. Whether variables are global or local is a informed guess made by Python. An assumption is made that any variable is local which has been assigned a value in a function. Therefore, for assigning a value to a global variable inside a function, the global statement needs to be used first. The statement *global VarName*tells that VarName is global. Searching the local namespace for the variable is stopped by Python.

The dir( ) function-

It returns a systematic list of strings consisting of the names defined by a module. List consists of all the functions, modules and variables that are defined in a module.

The globals( ) and locals( ) functions-

These functions can be used to return names in the local and local namespaces depending on the location from where they are called. If from inside a function a globals( ) is called, it will return all the names that can be globally accessed from that function. In case locals( ) is called from inside a function, it will return names that can be locally accessed from that function. The return type for both the functions is dictionary. So the names can be extracted using the keys( ) function.

The reload( ) function

The code in the top level portion of a module is executed only once when the module is imported into a script. However, if you want to execute the top level code again, then use the reload( ) function. A previously imported module is imported again by this function.

Syntax –

reload(module_name)

In syntax, *module_name* is the name of the module to be reloaded and not the string consisting of the module name.

CLASSES

As we know that Python is an object-oriented language, therefore using and creating objects and classes is easy. A class is a user-defined model for an object that defines a set of attributes that portray any object of the class. The attributes are the data members and methods, associated via dot notation. Data member is an instance variable or a class variable that holds data related with a class and its objects. The instance variable is a variable that is defined inside a method and belongs to the current instance of a class.

How to create classes?

A new class definition is created by a *class* statement. The name of the class straight away follows the keyword *class* followed by a colon.

class ClassName:

'Optional class documentation string'

class_suite

- A class has a documentation string, which can be accessed via ClassName._doc_.
- Each component statement that defines class members, functions and data attributes exist in the *class_suite.*

How to create instances of class?

Use class name to call the class and pass in no matter what arguments its *_init_* method accepts for creating an instance of a class.

How to access attributes?

Dot operator with object need to be used in order to access the object's attributes.

Built-in class attributes

Dot operator can be used to access the built-in attributes–

a) _dict_ - dictionary containing class's namespace
b) _name_ - class name
c) _doc_ - class documentation string or none, if undefined.
d) _bases_ - probably a vacant tuple containing the base classes in the order of their occurrence in the base class list.

e) _module_ - the module name in which class is defined. This attribute in interactive mode is "_main_".

Garbage Collection

In Python, to make the memory space free, objects (class instances or built-in) that are not required are deleted automatically. Garbage collection is a method by which Python from time to time recovers memory blocks that are no longer in use. Python's garbage collector runs while the program is being executed and is triggered when an object's reference count reaches zero. An object's reference count increases when it is positioned in a container (tuple, list or dictionary) or is assigned a new name. The object's reference count decreases when it is deleted with *del,* its reference goes out of scope or it is reassigned. Python automatically collects when an object's reference count reaches zero.

Class inheritance

A pre-existing class can be used for deriving and creating a new class instead of begining from scratch by listing the parent class after the new class name inside parentheses. The attributes of its parent class are inherited by the child class, and these attributes can be used as if they were defined in the child class. Just like their parent class the derived classes can be declared. Though, after the class name a list of base classes to inherit from is given.

Syntax –

class SubClassName (ParentClass1[, ParentClass2,. . .]):

'Optional class documentation string'

class_suite (Python - Environment Setup)

Chapter 6: Exception handling

Exception

An event that interrupts the standard flow of the program's instructions at the time of execution is called as an exception. Typically, when such a situation is encountered by a Python script that it cannot handle, it raises an exception. In other words, an exception is a Python object that depicts an error. When an exception is raised in Python script, it either the exception is handled immediately or it is terminated.

How to handle an exception?

In case you find a suspicious code in a program, then the program can be defended by putting that code in a **try:** block. After this include an **except:**statement followed by a block of code which manages the problem as gracefully as possible.

Syntax –

try:

You do your operations here;

....

except Exception I:

If there is Exception I, then execute this block.

Except Exception II:

If there is Exception II, then execute this block.

....

else:

If there is no exception then execute this block.

Please note –

- A single try statement can have multiple except statements.
- A generic except clause can also be provided, which manages any exception.
- An else-clause can also be included after except clause(s). If the code in try: block does not raise an exception the code in the else-block is executed.
- A better place for code that does not need the try: block's protection is the else-block.

Except Clause with no exception –all the exceptions that occur are caught by the try-except statement. However, it doesn't make the programmer recognize the root cause of the problem that may occur.

Except clause with multiple exceptions- the same except statement to handle multiple exceptions can be used.

Try-finally clause – The finally: block with try: block can be used. In the finally block you can place any code that must execute, irrespective of the fact that the try-block has raised an exception or not.

Argument of an exception – An argument is a value that gives more information about the problem and an exception can have an argument. You can catch an exception's argument by providing a variable in the except clause.

Raising Exceptions

You can raise exceptions in several ways by using the raise statement.

Syntax –

raise [Exception [, args [, traceback]]]

Here, *argument* is a value for the exception argument and *Exception* is the type of exception. However, argument is optional; if not supplied, the exception argument is None. For example, an exception can be a class, string or an object. Most exceptions that Python core raises are classes, with an argument that is an instance of the class.

In Python, you are allowed to create your own exceptions by deriving classes from the standard built-in exceptions. (Python Exceptions Handeling)

Conclusion

This brings us to the end of this edition of the book. We can easily say that Python is a powerful language and that is the reason why all big companies are looking for programmers who have the knowledge of this dynamic language.

Before we end, let's summarize on what we have learned so far. The book began with basic introduction to Python, its features, how to install and set up. We also understood that Python has fewer syntactical constructs thus making it easy and readable. All Python fundamentals i.e. variables, data types, operators, lists, strings, loops, tuples and dictionary have been covered in the book.

We have also ensured that the concept of function, classes, and modules is covered for a better understanding of the language. The last section on exception handling can be useful in practical application.

To conclude, we can say that once you are clear on the basics of Python you will be able to create almost anything you want.

Thank you once again for downloading this book, hope it has given you a meaningful insightinto Python.

Works Cited

Python - Environment Setup. n.d. 2017. <https://www.tutorialspoint.com/python/python_environment.htm>.

Python Exceptions Handeling. n.d. 2017. <https://www.tutorialspoint.com/python/python_exceptions.htm>.

.

Book 5

XML Crash Course

By: PG WIZARD BOOKS

Step By Step Guide To Mastering Python Programming!

XML Crash Course: Step by Step Guide To Mastering XML Programming!

XML Crash Course: Step by Step Guide To Mastering XML Programming!

Table of Contents

XML Crash Course: Step by Step Guide To Mastering XML Programming!

Introduction

When it comes to getting into the world of coding and all the programming that you would like to do, there are many options that you are able to choose from. Some choose to work with options like Java and HTML so that they can create projects online and on web pages that really wow. Others like to go with Python because it is an easy one for beginners to work with. But a great coding language that you can learn to work with and which we are going to discuss inside this guidebook, is the XML coding language.

You will notice as you go through this guidebook that there are some similarities that come up between the XML language and the HTML language. While both of these are similar, there are some differences that come up and we will talk about these inside of this guidebook. We will also spend some time talking about some of the basics of XML, some of the parts that you would want to add into the code to make things easier, how to declare XML documents (which is something optional you are able to do to make the code work a bit better) and even how to work with the different character entities to help make coding easier. These are just a few of the things that we will discuss in order to get you familiar with the XML code so that you can use it on your own.

When you are ready to get started on a new coding language and you want to pick one of the very best that is also easy for beginners to work with, you should learn how to use XML. This guidebook is going to give you the best results to ensure that you will learn everything that you need to know in order to start with the XML language.

Chapter 1: What is XML Programming?

When it comes to learning a new programming language, there are so many choices and it can all seem a bit overwhelming. You want to make sure that you are picking choices that will get you ahead and will make it easier to work on the systems and programs that you want, but with all of the choices that are out there, how are you going to be able to choose the one that is right for you. There are choices for beginners and ones for those who want to be a bit more advanced. There are choices that are great for working on websites while others are good for a specific operating system or for working inside of your business statistics. There really isn't a right or wrong answer, you just need to take the time to look at the different options and find the one that is right for you.

In this guidebook, we are going to take a look at the XML program. This one stands for Extensible Markup Language and it is one of the most talked about programming languages, only second to Java, because of all the great things that you are able to work with. inside of this language, you are able to store, organize, and identify your information with the help of tags. If you have used Java or JavaScript programming in the past, you may have heard about HTML tags, but these two are not quite the same. The XML language is not one that is going to replace HTML later on down the road, but it does introduce some new possibilities because it uses some of the features of HTML.

So, to make this easy, the XML program is going to be software and hardware independent and it is often used in order to carry information. even though the markup that is used will look similar to what you are finding with HTML, you will see that these are two different entities. For example, XML is set up to focus on the data that you are using while HTML is more focused on the appearance of your data. XML is going to describe your data while the HTML is going to display the data when you are done.

To make this work better, let's take a look at a good example of how this will work. Keep in mind that you will need to define some of your own tags because these are not predefined inside of XML. Here is the example:

```
<note>
```

```
<to>Jane</to>

<from<John</from>

<heading>Memo</heading>

<body>Come to the meeting at ten in the morning tomorrow</body>

</note>
```

With this example, you are probably able to tell what is going on. The information is there for both the sender as well as the receiver and there are headings and a body message that you will be able to use. But remember that the XML document is basically going to contain the information that you want along with some tags. There are no specific functions that go with it. On its own, XML is going to be pretty useless until you get the right software program in there to turn it into something.

Now basically, you are going to have three characteristics that come with the XML language that you are able to use and you can remember these by thinking about the name of the program. The three characteristics that you can work with include:

Extensible: this means that the XML program is going to allow you the change to characterize your own tags so that they will work with your application. You will also be able to extend the concept of the document, which is usually a file that is going to live on the server. It can also be a piece of data that is temporary and will flow between the various web servers.

Markup: this it eh elements or the tags that are familiar inside of XML. The elements that you are creating in this language will be similar to the ones in HTML, but you will be able to define the elements or tags that you want.

Language: the languages that are used inside of HTML and XML are pretty similar, but there is some more flexibility when using XML. You are able to use it to create and define some other languages rather than just having it set in stone like HTML.

Do I really need to learn how to use XML?

Many people wonder if it is worth their time to learn how to use XML since it is so similar to what you will find in HTML. You do need XML because there are times when you would like to create and deal with the data. The HTML document is just going to display the information; it is not going to work with it to make it look nicer or anything else.

In addition, working with XML allows you to use different contexts that are not just found on the web, including applications and web services. Any time that you would like to organize your data and send it over to another person, without having to worry about all the displays like you would find with HTML, the XML language is going to be the one to work with.

Downloading the XML language

Before we go any further in this guidebook and learn how to write some codes (as well as some of the other cool things that you are able to do in this language), we are going to need to take some time to get all of this downloaded onto the computer. The XML language is from Microsoft and at the time of this book, the XML Parser 3.0 is the option that we are going to use for our projects.

First, you need to make sure that the operating system and computer are the right kind to run this. To work with the XML Parser 3.0, you will need to have a Windows computer that is Windows 2000, Windows Server 2003, or Windows XP. You can then go to the Microsoft website to find this version, or a newer version, of the XML program an download it to your computer. Read through the prompts that come up on your screen until you get don with the download and it is all installed on your computer. At this point, you are ready to get started with some coding!

Chapter 2: Learning the Basic Syntax of XML

Now that we have the right program on our computer and ready to go, it is time to learn a bit about the syntax of a code in XML. If you learn the basic syntax of your code, it is going to be much easier to write more complex codes later on. Of course, with the options that we are going to talk about in this chapter, we are going to keep things pretty simple to start, but as you learn more about XML, it is pretty easy to add in the other parts that you will want to learn.

Below we are going to write out a basic syntax that you are able to use in this language and then we will take some time to discuss the different parts so that is makes sense for what you are doing. Here is the basic syntax that you can use:

```
<?xmlersio="1.0^)>
<contact-info>
<name>Manny Dunphy</name>
<company>Real Realtor</company>
<phone>(895) 444-1111</phone>
</contact-info>
```

As you can see with this example there are several parts of information that are placed inside. You need to make sure that the right syntax is used and the right symbols, so that the compiler has an idea of what you would like to send. This is a pretty simple option that will have the contact information for this person, Manny Dunphy, who works with Real Realtor as well as their phone number. You can expand this out as much as you would like or keep it this simple.

Remember than when working in XML, we are concentrating on the data, and collecting the data, rather than worrying about how the data is going to look. If you plan on putting this kind of information into a website or you want to make sure that it looks nice, you are going to need to work with the HTML format to make this happen.

Working with XML declarations

When it comes to XML, there are some documents that are going to have declarations and some that will not. If your document is one of them that has the declaration, here is a good example of how you would want to write it all out:

```
<?xmlv version="1.0" encoding="UTF-8"?>
```

For this one, the version is going to be the XML version and the other specific encoding is going to tell the document that you are going to use character encoding for this particular project. As we go through some of the other parts that you are able to work on in this book, you will see some more of the XML declaration and it is going to make a bit more sense to you.

Tags and Elements

Next on the list to work with are the elements and tags. The elements inside of XML are basically going to be the building blocks. They are going to be like a container that will hold many of the different parts of the XML ode, including media objects, attributes, elements, and text. Pretty much any element that comes into the code could be placed into the containers here. Each document is going to contain at least one element, but often there will be more if the code is longer. You can use the scopes in order to delimit using a start or end tag. Here is a good example of how you would write out the syntax for the elements and tags:

```
<element-name attribute1 attribute2>
...content
</element-name>
```

The element name in this example is the name that you would give to the element in this place. The name needs to be the same and matching in the beginning as well as in the ending tags. The attribute1 and attribute 2 are the element attributes that are going to be separated by some white space. You will be able to use the attributes in order to refer to a property of the element and often it is going to be associated with not only a name inside the code, but also with a certain value that you assign.

Writing out a comment inside of XML

There are times when you would like to leave a little comment inside of the code. When it comes to coding, the comments are just messages that the compiler is going to skip over and not read, but which can be useful to you or the other programmers who would like to go through the code. You will find that the syntax for writing out comments inside of XML is going to be the same as doing so in HTML. You will be able to use this syntax in order to write out your comment:

<!—An example of a comment→

Comments will need to all be done in this manner to tell the compiler when to start and stop the comment. When the compiler sees this, it will just skip over to the next part of the code, without causing any delays or issues in the code. You are able to add in as many of these comments as you would like or feel that you need in the code to make things easier, but you should be careful to not add in too many or you will end up with a messy code.

Starting a new line inside of XML

There are times when you will want to get started on a new line in XML. When it comes to doing this in applications of Windows, the new line is going to be done with the carriage return and line feed. On the old MAC systems, the new line is going to be with the carriage return and in Unix it is going to be the line feed. But when you are using XML, this is all going to be done with the line feed. You are able to start a new line in the code when you need to keep things in order and to make it easier to read through the code.

Unlike what you are going to find with HTML, the XML code is going to see white spaces a bit different. While you are able to have several whitespaces in a row on

HTML, you will not have this inside of XML. Instead, if you have more than one whitespace in a row, the XML program is going to take these and turn them into just one.

These are just some of the basics that you are able to use when it comes to working in the XML coding language. They are going to help you to form some of the basics of your code and can come in use later on when you are ready to write out some more complicated codes. Make sure to learn some of these basics to make it easier for code writing later on and to further understand how the XML code will work for you.

Chapter 3: Declaring Inside of XML

We discussed the XML declaration a bit earlier on, but now we are going to break this down a bit in order to help it make more sense for you to use. The XML declaration is going consist of the details that you need to put in order by an XML processor to break down and analyze the document of XML. This is an optional feature that you can choose to either use or not use, however, when you do choose to use it, you will notice that it occurs right at the beginning of the document. Here is the syntax that you can use for XML declaration to make things a bit easier to use.

```
<?xml
	Version="version_nmuber"
	Encoding="encoding_delcaration"
	Standalone="standalone_status"
?>
```

Each of the parameters that you are going to use will have their own name so keep these in line and then an equal sign as well as a value. You are able to set up the numbers, rather than the quotes, to get the code to react in the way that you would like. There are a few rules that you will need to keep in mind when you are declaring inside of XML and these rules include the following:

- If there is a declaration inside of XML, you will need to make sure that you position it as the first line in your document. If you put it somewhere else inside of the document, you are going to run into some issues.
- When working with a declaration inside of XML, you will need to have a version number attribute to help make it work.
- The names and the parameter values that you set are going to be case sensitive, and it is recommended that while working inside of XML you keep the names in the lower case.

- There is a proper order that you are going to use with the parameter name to ensure that the compiler will read it properly. The proper order includes version, encoding, and then standalone, just like you will see with the example that we gave above.
- You get to choose the quote type that you use, either the single or the double quotes. Just make sure that this stays consistent in the code.
- You will also notice that in this declaration, you will not need to have a closing tag like you do in some of the other coding that you will work with.
- If you are doing an encoding declaration, this is going to be a bit different, but for the rest of the declaration, you will need to keep it all in lower case letters.
- If you find that there are attributes, entities, and elements that are referenced or defined by an external DTD, your standalone is going to equal "no".

So now that we know a few of the rules that go with XML declaration, let's take a look at how you would do this in the code to get a better feel for it. This example is going to have all of the parameters defined for us.

```
<?xml> version='1.0' encoding='iso-8859-1' standalone='no'?>
```

And that is all there is to declaring inside of XML. Any time that you would need to do this inside of your code, you can just use this simple syntax, and then add in the information that you would like inside. This makes it easy for you to get the results that you want and as you can see, this only takes up about a line of code (maybe a little more depending on the declaration that you are using) and then you are all set.

Chapter 4: Working with Character Entities and Comments in XML

We talked about comments and some of the characters that you would use in XML a little bit before, but now we need to take this a step further and start to work on how the comments and the characters are going to work when it is time to actually write the code that you would like. When it comes to working with comments inside of XML, you will notice that they are similar to the comments that you have in HTML. They are basically little notes that are added into the code that will help you and other programmers to understand what is going on in the code, but will have absolutely no effect on how the code will work when it runs. One thing to note when writing out a comment is that you shouldn't try to nest one comment inside of another, because this will just cause a mess and could bring up an error inside of the code. Here is an example of a code that would have a comment in it (take the time to write this in your compiler to get some good practice).

```
<?xml version="1.0" encoding="UTF-8"?>

<!—Test scores are uploaded by grade -→

<class_list>

        <student>

        <name>Lilly</name>

        <grade>B+</grade>

        </student>

        </class_list>
```

Of course, this is a pretty simple example that just has one student and it is likely that you would add in a few more to fill this out but it is a good look at how the comment would be able to work inside of the code. It explains that the test scores were going to be upgraded by the grade that you were using and since we only used one it was not the most important, but if you had a lot of other students in here, it would show up. Remember that you are able to add in as many of these comments as you would like, you just need to be careful about using the right symbols to tell the compiler what you are doing.

Character Entities

The entity of the XML document is going to be the root of the entity tree and it is really the starting point for the processor. It can also be seen as the placeholder. The entities are going to be acknowledged being in the document prolog or in the DTD and they will often work with symbols that are only used for the entities and never for the content inside the code. For example, the < and > symbols are only used for the closing and the opening and the character entities are going to be used to make these visible.

Types of character entities

There are a number of character entities that you will be able to use inside of your code including the following:

Predefined character entities

These character entities are going to be introduced in order to prevent the ambiguity that can come when certain symbols are used. For example, there could be some issues when the (<) and (>) symbols are used along with the angle tags of (<>). The character entities are going to help delimit tags. You are able to use some of the following tags in order to get the right results in your code without showing all of the ambiguity at the same time:

Greater than: >

Less than: <

Ampersand: &

Single quote: &apos

Double quote: &wuot

Numerical character entities

With this entity, we are going to use numbers in order to reference and define the character entity that we want to use. We are able to choose numbers that are in decimal and hexadecimal format. There are lots of numeric references that you are able to use, and sometimes there can be too many for you to remember. The numeric reference is a number that is found in the Unicode character set. The syntax that you are going to be able to use for the decimal number reference inside of XML includes:

&# decimal number.

And then when you would like to use the hexadecimal reference, you would go with the following syntax:

&#x Hexadecimal number

Named character references

Wile the numerical character entities are a great way to get started, remember all of these numbers can be really hard, especially as a beginner who is just getting started with coding. This is why most people are going to use the name character entity instead to make things a little easier. There are a number of different ways that you can name the actions that you want to do inside of your code with the name character references, but here are a few of the examples that you can try:

- Acute: this one is going to refer to a capital A character that will have an acute accent on it.
- Ugrave; this is the name of the small u that has a grave accent.

Character entities and types are important when it comes to working inside of your code. They are going to help you to give the assignments to your work, whether you choose to use the numeric or one of the other choices. You can pick out the one that is right for you to work on your XML code.

Chapter 5: Processing and Encoding Inside Your XML Document

In this chapter, we are going to spend some time working on processing and encoding inside of your document. When you choose to work with processing instructions, you are allowing the documents to contain instructions for every application. You should know that these processes and the instructions are not going to be included in the character data that we talked about in the previous chapter, but they will still need to be able to pass through the application that you are creating.

The processing instructions will allow you to pass on the information that you would like to all of the different applications. You are able to place these in any location of the document that you would like. In fact, you are also able to place them into the prolog, which could include the document type definition or DTD, or at the end of the document as the textual content. The syntax to use in order to make this happen includes:

```
<?target instructions?>
```

For this syntax, the target is going to be responsible for recognizing the application from which the instruction comes from. You will be able to place the name of any application that you would like to use to tell the program where the instructions are located to use. And then the part of the instructions is going to be used in order to describe any of the information that you would like the application to process in order to finish it out.

The processing instructions are not used all that often because of the specialties that come with it. But if you do choose to work with these processing instructions, you will use them in order to link your XML document to a style sheet. In order to make this happen, you would need to type out the following type of syntax:

```
<?xml-stylesheet href= "businessforms.css" type="text/css"?>
```

These are basically the instructions that your target application is going to process inside of the XML document. With this particular instruction, the browser is going to be able to get the browser to recognize the right target by initiating that XML document and that it should transform it before it is shown. Notice that the first attribute comes out as the type of XSL that you are trying to transform and then the second attribute is going to indicate the location of the type you are transforming.

Working with XML encoding

Now that we have talked a bit about using processing inside of the XML document, it is time to work on the encoding inside of your documents. The process of encoding inside of XML is to convert the Unicode characters that you are trying to use into binary ones. The moment that the processor for XML reads a specific document, it is going to immediately encode the document according to the encoding type that you pick to go with it. There are different types of coding that you are able to use and we are going to look at them a bit more below:

Types of encoding

Inside of the XML code, there are gong to be two types of encoding that you are able to use, the UTF-8 and UTF16. They can both be used in separate ways in the coding that you work on. But if you end up not picking out the encoding that you would like to use with your XML document, the default is going to be the UTF-8. The syntax that you are going to use will depend on the type of encoding that you are using. For the UTF-8, you would use the following syntax:

```
<?xml version="1.0" encoding="UTF-8" standalone="no"?>
```

And then the syntax that you would need to use for the UTF-16 encoding would include:

```
<?xml version="1.0" encoding="UTF-16" standalone="no"?>
```

As you can see, these are going to be pretty similar, you will just put in the different options that you are able to use for the encoding. You will just need to pick the one that is best for you or choose to leave it blank so that the UTF-8 is going to be picked by default. Here is a good example of using the encoding of UTF-8:

```
<?xml version="1.0" encoding="UTF-8" standalone="no"?>
<contact-info>
        <name>Dunny Bobbins</name>
        <company>Real Realtors</company>
        <phone>(553) 512 1123</phone>
</contact-info>
```

With this example, we are using the UTF-8 encoding, as you are able to see by looking at that part of the code. This means that the 8-bit characters are the ones that you will use. For the most part, you would use this option when you want to have files that are encoded to be smaller because you are just going with 8 bits or smaller. If you don't care as much about the size of the file or you would like to get it to be bigger, the UTF-16 is going to be the option that you should use for your encoding.

And that is all there is to the encoding process. It is simple to use and will ensure that the document is going through the right processes to work properly. You can choose to go with either the UTF-8 or the UTF-16 based on your needs, but most of the time the UTF-8 is the best one to choose to go with and if you don't place an option into the code, you are going to find that the processor will choose to go with the UTF-8 by default.

Chapter 6: Working with the Elements and Tags

Earlier we spent some time talking about the elements and tags inside of the XML document, but we are going to now spend a bit more time on this to see how they actually work inside the code and how you can get them to work for your needs. When you are working inside of the XML program, tags are going to be one of the most vital parts. They are the foundation to your language because they are able to do so many things. You will be able to use them as a method to define the scopes of your elements, insert special instructions, declare settings necessary for parsing environments, and to insert comments. There are several different types of tags that you are able to use in XML and they are categorized by this:

Start tag

The start tag is the one that you will use in order to start all of the elements in XML that are non empty. You would be able to write it out similar to this: <address>

Empty tag

Another type of tag that you are going to use is an empty tag. In between the start tag and the end tag (which we are going to talk about soon), is the text that you are going to write out, or the content, of the code. If your element ends up not having any content, you will find that the tag is considered empty. There are a few ways that you are able to represent the empty elements that you are working with.

To start, if you would like to have an end tag that comes right after your start tag, you would just write it out like this "<hr> </hr>". You are also able to have an element tag that is completely empty such as writing out "<hr />". You are able to use these empty element tags for any of the elements inside of the code that aren't going to contain any content inside of them.

The end tag

In addition to the two types of tags that we have been discussing so far, you can also work with the end tag. This is just as necessary as working with the start tag because it tells the code when that particular part is all done or not. You would have a simple syntax to write out in order to make this happen, including </address>. This is going to be the complement to working with the start tag and you will need to have both of these in place inside of the code. Keep in mind that it will need to have the (/) symbol in front of it in order to prevent confusion and to help end out that part of the card.

Some of the rules for using tags in XML

Sometimes it can be a good idea to know the rules about the tags before you get too far into this process. This will help to speed things up and ensure that you are going to get the best results. Unlike some of the other languages that you will work with inside of coding, XML is going to be considered case sensitive. This basically means that you are going to have to take note and be careful when you are using upper case and lower case letters. The tags that you are creating inside of XML will need to be either all upper case letter or all lower case letters. You will find that a simple mistake in this field is going to give you some bad results, so always make sure to review each of the codes that you will use before finalizing them.

For example, if you typed into the code <address> and then ended it as </Address>, the code is going to have some troubles with these. The XML is going to see them as different because of the capitalization that comes with it, and it will start to treat this code as an erroneous syntax. In order to get this error fixed, you would have to change the ending tag so that it was lower case rather than the upper case that was used.

Another rule that you will need to keep track of when using your tags in XML is that you need to close them properly. For example, if you have a tag that is opened up inside of another element, you will need to make sure that it has been closed before the external element is all closed up.

When it comes to naming the tags that you will use, you need to be careful to get them the right way. For example, make sure that you are doing a good job of picking out the upper case and lower case letters and keeping them consistent when naming things is important. You also are not able to use any form of XML, regardless of the case that you are using, because it is going to confuse the processor and how it should behave. You can add in letters, digits, hyphens, underscores, and periods inside of the names of the elements. However, if you are using punctuation inside of this code, you are only able to use the underscore, hyphen, and period. The names of the elements are not able to have spaces. Outside of these simple rules, you are able to use any name that you would like to name the tags of your code.

Elements that are used in XML

Next on the list to explore are the elements that are inside of XML. The elements are kind of like the building blocks of the language, the part that is going to be built up on the foundation of the tags. These elements are great to work as containers that hold many things such as media objects, elements, attributes, and text and often they are going to hold many of these at once. Any of the documents that you work with inside of XML will have at least one of these elements, but the longer ones will hold more. For empty elements, the scopes will be delimited with the help of an empty element tag, but for the ones that have elements inside of them, the scopes are going to be delimited with the help of a start tag and an end tag.

Writing out the syntax of the element can be pretty easy, but here is a simple example to help you get it started:

```
<element-name attribute1 attribute2>
Whatever content you would like to add into here.
</element-name>
```

With the example above, the element name is going to be whatever name you would like to give the element in this case and then the attribute 1 and the attribute 2 are going to be the attributes that you give to your element, and they will be divided up with some white space. The attribute word is going to pretty much define the property of the element. It is going to work by associating the name back to the corresponding value, which is typically going to be a string of characters. When you would like to write out the attribute, you will simply write it out as name=”value” and that is it.

When you are working on writing out the name of your element, take the time to see that the name you use in the start tag will be the same as the name that you place into the end tag. In addition, the word name should have an equal sign with it, as well as a string value that is inside of either double quotes or single quotes.

What about the empty element?

So above we were talking about a code that has an element inside of it. But there are times when you will have an empty element. Basically, the empty element is going to be an element that doesn’t have content in it. When you are writing the syntax for this one, you would need to use the following format to tell the processor what to do:

```
<name attribute1 attribute2.../>
```

If you are trying to create a new document and you will need to use a variety of elements, the following format is going to be the best:

```
<?xml version = “1.0”?>

<contact-information>

<address category = “home”>

<name> Wendy Dawn </name>

<office> My Office </office>

<phone> (632) 246 1234 </phone>
```

```
<address/>
</contact-information>
```

Working with elements and tags inside of the XML document is one of the best things that you are able to do for your code. These are going to help you to get everything in place and they are the foundation and the building blocks that you really need inside of your code. It can take some time to learn the different things that you need inside of these, but when you are able to bring it all together, these are the two parts of the code that you need in order to really get it started the right way.

Chapter 7: Viewers and Editors in XML

Inside of XML, there are several methods that you are able to use in order to view documents. For example, you are able to use a browser in order to view a document, or you can choose to go with a simple text editor. Most of the browsers that are available will support XML, so this shouldn't be a worry. Or you can choose to just click on the files for XML and get them to open up; but remember that this is only going to work if the XML file is a local one. If the file is one that is found on your server, you just need to type in the right URL path into the address bar, just like when you want to open up some of the other files on your browser.

As mentioned, there are many ways that you are able to look and view the XML documents at any time that you would like and the method that you choose is going to be a personal decision. Some of the options include:

XML text editors: there are many text editors that you are able to use and you can make the decision that is right for you. Notepad, TextEdit, and Textpad are great options to work with to create and view documents in XML, but other options will work as well.

Google Chrome: while all browsers are going to work well with XML, this one is really good to work with. there seems to be few problems with using it and it makes it easy to open up the XML code you want to use.

Mozilla Firefox: this one is also a good browser to use, but you do need to first open the code in Google Chrome. To do this, you need to take the file and double click on it in order to see the code displayed in some colorful text. This is a good thing because it makes it easier to read the code. Then at the left portion of the element, you will see a plus and a minus sign. If you click on the plus sign, the code is going to expand but if you click on the minus sign, you will see that the code hides.

Errors in my document

There are times when there will be some errors in your XML documents. If you notice that the code is missing out on certain tags, there are some errors that are going to show up. If there is an error somewhere in the code, you are going to get a message that should contain some information about the error that you are dealing with. sometimes it is something simple such as misspelling a word or using lower case in the start tag and then upper case in the end tag. You will need to double check your code to see what the issue is so that you can make some changes to the code.

Editors in XML

When you are working inside of XML, you are going to need to work with an editor of some sort. The editor is going to be useful to create, as well as make changes, in the document that you are using. There are many different editors that you are bale to use and most of them are free and may even come on your computer already, so this can make things easier. For example, Notepad or Wordpad are two great options that you can use, or you can download a professional editor to use from online. The online editors are a bit more powerful and sometimes beginners like to go with them because they do some of the work, such as close tags that you leave open, check the syntax, and highlight the syntax in color so that it is easier to read. You can make the decision about what kind you would like to use and the features that you think will be the most helpful when you are learning how to code.

Conclusion

Working with a new coding language is something that can take some time and effort. You want to be able to get the most out of the language, but you also don't want to waste your time on something that is too hard to learn and understand. This guidebook is going to take a bit of time to discuss the XML coding language, how to use it and why you would want to learn this particular language.

Inside this guidebook, you are going to learn everything you need in order to do well with the XML code. We are going to start out with some of the basics that come with XML coding, such as what it is and how it varies from HTML (even though both of them are pretty similar) and then move on to some of the special parts that are found inside of your first code so that you can become more familiar with it all. Then we move on how you would declare inside of XML (which is something that is optional and you can choose to do or not) along with working in comments and special characters' amount other topics.

There is so much that you are able to do with the XML code once you take the time to learn this code and what all you can do with it. When you are ready to get started in coding or you are looking for a new code that you can work with, make sure to take some time to look through this guidebook and get the most out of the XML code.

www.ingramcontent.com/pod-product-compliance
Lightning Source LLC
Chambersburg PA
CBHW071434180526
45170CB00001B/348

* 9 7 8 1 5 4 5 1 8 5 8 4 1 *